Paul C. Holinger,
M.D., M.P.H.,
PROFESSOR OF PSYCHIATRY
AT RUSH-PRESBYTERIAN-
ST. LUKE'S MEDICAL CENTER
AND
FACULTY, TRAINING/
SUPERVISING ANALYST
AT THE CHICAGO INSTITUTE
FOR PSYCHOANALYSIS,

WITH
Kalia Doner

*The Nine Signals
Infants Use to
Express Their
Feelings*

What
Babies Say
Before
They Can
Talk

A FIRESIDE BOOK
Published by Simon & Schuster
New York London Toronto Sydney Singapore

FIRESIDE
Rockefeller Center
1230 Avenue of the Americas
New York, NY 10020

Photographs included on pages 10, 118, 123, 141, 154, 155, 158, 163,
177, and 212 are © 2003 Paul C. Holinger, M.D.
Photographs included on pages 10, 126, 133, 146, 152, 158, 165, 199,
and 211 are © Retrofile.com.
Original artwork on page 35 © 2003 Jeremy Sherer Oberle

FIRESIDE and colophon are registered trademarks of Simon & Schuster, Inc.

For information regarding special discounts for bulk purchases,
please contact Simon & Schuster Special Sales at 1-800-456-6798
or business@simonandschuster.com

Designed by Christine Weathersbee

Manufactured in the United States of America

10   9   8   7   6   5   4   3   2   1

Library of Congress Cataloging-in-Publication Data
Holinger, Paul C.
    What babies say before they can talk : the nine signals infants use to express
their feelings / Paul C. Holinger, with Kalia Doner.
        p. cm.
    Includes bibliographical references and index.
    1. Nonverbal communication in infants. 2. Interpersonal communication
in infants. I. Doner, Kalia. II. Title.
BF720.C65H64 2003
155.42'2369—dc21   2003049033

ISBN 0-7434-0667-2

Dedicated,
of course,
to Joni
and
to Campbell

If we could first know where we are,
and whither we are tending, we could better judge
what to do, and how to do it.
—ABRAHAM LINCOLN,
THE "HOUSE DIVIDED" SPEECH, 1858

. . . we are always slow in admitting great changes
of which we do not see the steps.
—CHARLES DARWIN,
The Origin of Species, 1859

The trouble you don't get into,
you don't have to get out of.
—HELEN C. BOYDEN,
DEERFIELD ACADEMY

Acknowledgments

I AM PROFOUNDLY GRATEFUL TO THE FOLLOWING PERSONS WHO were kind enough to read parts or all of this manuscript. Their thoughtful observations and suggestions were invaluable. So, thanks again to: Kim Coleman, Lisa Considine, Donna and Michael DeCaigny, Marsha Fenton, Michael Ferkol, Marlene Goodfriend, Richard and Tia Holinger, Philip Linke, Mel and Mary Marks, Alan and Claire Martin, Barbara Miner, Jill Simmons Mueller, Phil and Mariette Orth, Karen Pierce, Gary Rosenmutter, Paul Rubin, K. O. Rutherford, Meg Schneider, Joan Gately Shapiro, Tracy Sherrod, Abigail Sivan, Diane Stevens, Don and Nancy Tubesing, Nancy Vert, participants in the 2002 class on affect at the Chicago Institute for Psychoanalysis (including James Anderson, Alice Bernstein, Diane Dean, Christine Kieffer, Jackie Marton, and Frank Summers), and members of the Faculty Seminar in the Department of Psychiatry at Rush-Presbyterian-St. Luke's Medical Center. I am especially indebted to Donald Nathanson, for his assistance with both content and photographs; Cherise Grant, editor at Simon & Schuster, who was essential to this project in so many ways; and Michele Mabbs and William Funchion, whose detailed help and encouragement were of inestimable importance.

I am extremely fortunate to have so many colleagues and friends who provided guidance, support, and education throughout the years this book was in progress. I owe my sincerest gratitude to Michael Basch, Helen Beiser, Barbara and Mark Berger, Pam Cantor, Barry Childress, Bert Cohler, Virginia Demos, Stuart Edelman, Hank Evans, Gail Fahey, Jan Fawcett, Robert Galatzer-Levy, Ben Garber, Arnold and Connie Goldberg, Roy R. Grinker, Jr., Michael Grover, Miriam Gutmann, Irving Harris, Herb Hendin, George Higgins, Ann Kaplan, Jerry Kavka and the Library of the Chicago Institute for Psychoanalysis, Elaine Klemen, Charles Kligerman, Sue and Craig Manske, Michael McConnell, Betty Melton, Amy and Dan Meyer, Jack and Kerry Kelly Novick, Roger Oberle, Dan and Margie Offer, participants of the Tuesday Meeting for Child Psychoanalysis, Susan Peterson, Cynthia Pfeffer, Barrie Richmond, Jackie Rivet-River, Fred Robbins, Barbara Rocah, Henry Seidenberg, Lou Shapiro, Howard Sudak, Sam Weiss, Cliff Wilkerson, Andy and Susan Williams, Edward and Gloria Wolpert, Glorye Wood, and Judy Zito.

A number of people were uniquely helpful in the development of this book through their caregiving, nurturing, and teaching. I thank you all so very much: Rita Anderson, Mike and Susan Brown, Matt Bryant, the Cade family, Ann Carr, Joanna Chang, Rosa Cordero, Patricia Crylan, Wendy Darnell, Andrea DeCook, Jennifer DeLong, Rachel Dobson, Tiffany Egan, Linda Feeney, Leila Fong, Amy Fumagalli, Pam Hagerman, Hinsdale Public Library, Carrie Hooper, Arlene Jarzab, Brooke Kelly, Stephanie Kessl, Betsy Klaric, Mary Lee Larsen, Susie Lebensorger, Madison Elementary School (Hinsdale, Illinois), Heather McBeth, Erin McKean, Melinda McMahon, David Matero, Kathy Muller, Julie O'Brien, Auggy Porreca, Susan Purser, Cira Sanchez, Mandy Satkamp, Nancy Schifo, Courtney Scukanec, Mary Sparks, Melissa Spencer, Kerry Tumbleson, and Barbara Wilson.

It is said that a picture is worth a thousand words—and this may be especially true when studying and playing with infants! For the opportunity to photograph and use pictures of their babies, I would like to thank the Clarke, DeCaigny, DeCook, Meyer, Richardson, and Zook families. I am very grateful to Jeremy Sherer Oberle for her original artwork. Thanks also to Campbell for his photographic assistance as well as for his contribution to the title.

To my patients, young and old, I owe a tremendous debt. Their courage and willingness to collaborate with me in grappling with their aspirations and apprehensions have granted me immeasurable learning and fulfillment.

To Regina Ryan, my agent, who was a believer in and skillful navigator of this project from the beginning, I am especially beholden. Her enthusiasm for the topic and her encouragement and perseverance were essential to the completion of this book.

To Kalia—wordsmith, colleague, and friend—I owe my deepest gratitude. Her patience, stamina, wisdom, good humor, willingness to learn and teach—all these attributes and more emerged during the course of this enterprise and endeared her to me.

I am particularly grateful to Cindy Wiertel, president of ABS Services. Her unswerving loyalty, willingness and ability to tackle new and different tasks, uncomplaining nature in the face of hard work, and logistical skills have been genuine blessings.

To my wife, Joni, and son, Campbell, all praise and love are truly due. You two made this book possible. I cannot thank you enough.

Paul C. Holinger, M.D.
Chicago, Illinois

Contents

Introduction

My Journey:
On the Road to Raising
Happy, Capable, Responsible Children

HUMAN BEINGS ARE BORN WITH A SET OF SIGNALS. CURRENT research suggests there are nine inborn signals: interest, enjoyment, surprise, distress, anger, fear, shame, disgust (a reaction to bad tastes), and dissmell (a reaction to bad odors). These are our earliest feelings. In time, these signals combine with each other and link up with experience to form our complex emotional life. Understanding these signals and how they work can make a world of difference for you and your baby. That is what this book is all about.

I'd like to introduce myself and describe how I came to be involved in the field of child development. I am a medical doctor, specializing in psychiatry and psychoanalysis. I enjoy sports, I love learning and, most important, I am the father of a ten-year-old boy. I think it is very important to help parents understand their children, so that these children might reach their full potential as happy, capable, responsible human beings.

From an early age, I've been interested in psychology—in part because as a child I had the sense that my well-meaning parents didn't understand what I was feeling. When I headed off to college I knew that I wanted to major in psychology and then go on to medical school and become a psychiatrist. I received my psychiatric training in Chicago, and then went to Harvard University School of Public Health in Boston to study psychiatric epidemiology—the study of the frequency and distribution of mental disorders. While in Boston, I became fascinated with the idea of prevention—rather than just treatment—of emotional problems. The theme of preventing emotional turmoil grew even stronger when I began treating adolescents and doing research on teenage violence and suicide. However, there was another piece to the puzzle. I returned to Chicago to set up practice and train in child and adult psychoanalysis. I wanted to understand the emotional life of children and adults in real depth and use that understanding to help my patients.

Since then I have worked with children as well as adult patients. Some patients require as many as five sessions a week. I have found that this kind of intense work allows patients to understand themselves and make progress in ways that no other kind of treatment provides. Yet, I have remained focused on preventing emotional suffering. I wondered: "What if I had been able to see Erik [a twenty-five-year-old patient], when he was five, and had worked with him and his parents then?" "What if I could have seen Margie's parents [a thirty-five-year-old woman with whom I worked four times per week for seven years with a very successful outcome] when she was an infant?" Could Erik and Margie have been spared the pain they struggled with as teenagers and adults?

I wondered how personalities were formed. I questioned how an individual's inborn attributes contribute to his or her emotional development and what role the environment—parents, caretakers, and social context—plays in the emergence of emotional problems later in life. I thought it was not enough to help troubled families and children, not because they can't be helped—they can make enormous progress in the quality of their lives—but because I felt compelled to find ways to prevent the problems from starting in the first place. I often recalled the words of Helen C. Boyden, a wonderful, wise woman who was my high school chemistry teacher: "The trouble you don't get into, you don't have to get out of!"

Remarkable successes have been achieved in the fields of psychiatry and psychoanalysis. However, in my opinion, we have come up short in two areas. First, we have not focused enough on prevention, and second, we have not done a good job of conveying to the public much of what is known in the area of child development. When talking about prevention of emotional problems, I am referring to the conflict, depression, and anxiety that can result from the misunderstanding and poor regulation of feelings; I am not referring to the major psychotic illnesses with biological components such as schizophrenia or bipolar disorder, although understanding these earliest feelings can help in those conditions as well. I hope my professional colleagues will appreciate that I am trying to convey in readable fashion various features of the preverbal affective world of the infant and caregiver and the tension-regulation issues involved.

During the twentieth century, research and clinical advances provided hope that prevention, not just treatment, of some aspects of emotional problems was possible. I immersed myself in data and theories about the way children's emotions develop and how they communicate their earliest feelings. A number of researchers such as Ainsworth, Bowlby, Demos, Emde, Greenspan, Lichtenberg, Main, Panksepp, Plutchik, Schore, Spitz, and Stern have made significant breakthroughs in understanding the development and neurobiology of human emotions, and clinicians such as Basch, Freud, Gedo, Goldberg, Kernberg, Kohut, Modell and Winnicott have made significant advances in treatment of emotional problems in children and adults. Ultimately, the conclusions in this book are based on five sources of data: clinical work with adult and children; studies of infants; research on evolution; brain investigations; and the findings of early intervention and prevention programs.

The study of human emotions is extremely complex, and many perspectives, theories, and data exist (for example, see Plutchik's *The Psychology and Biology of Emotion* and Panksepp's *Affective Neuroscience*, listed in the Resources section). However, throughout this book I will focus on three scientists and their work. These three have been particularly influential in my efforts to help parents raise happy, capable, responsible children.

The first scientist is Silvan Tomkins. Tomkins produced a four-volume work titled *Affect Imagery Consciousness*, which is an extensive exploration of emotional life. Tomkins and his colleagues Demos, Ekman, Izard, and Nathanson built on Darwin's work (e.g., *The Origin of Species; The Expression of the Emotions in Man and Animals*) and researched the inherited nature and development of human emotions. They concluded that all humans are born with biological responses to stimulation (affects, or signals), which provide for both communication and motivation, interact with each other, combine with experience, and determine how we act.

Daniel Stern, an infant researcher, is another major influence. His 1985 book *The Interpersonal World of the Infant* is a classic that changed how infancy is viewed. Stern emphasized that infants have significant social interactions from their earliest moments, and he demonstrated how parents' early validation of—and responses and attunement to—their children has a profound influence on the positive development of emotional life.

Lastly, Alexander Meltzoff's work has been a major influence on my thinking. Building on the earlier works of Darwin and Freud, Meltzoff and others have studied the tendencies of infants to identify with and imitate the important people in their lives. These complex research studies help us to understand the conscious and unconscious ways in which children become similar to and different from their parents.

During the time I was exploring emotions in infants and children, my wife and I had a son. As I spent time with other parents and their children, I found that the ideas of these researchers and clinicians made practical sense. All this information seemed to confirm that a child's emotional character—whether confident, inquisitive, optimistic, loving, and self-confident, or suspicious, pessimistic, and defensive—is formed by a complex web of influences made up of a child's genetic endowment, his earliest encounters with parents and the outside environment, and, later on, other experiences and developmental processes. But, most striking was my own realization that an understanding of the nine signals could make a positive difference in the development of the child's emotional life.

In my work, I saw that focusing on the child's signals could produce quite remarkable results. I remember a couple who stifled their five-year-old daughter's expressions of distress and anger. They shamed her into bottling them up, making her feel that she was a terrible child for feeling anger at all. As a result, their little daughter became quite obsessive and inhibited. I could have prescribed medication, but I thought that talking with her and her parents and trying to understand her thoughts and feelings would ultimately be of most help. So, I worked to help the parents appreciate that their child's signals for distress and anger were natural inborn responses hardwired in the brain and that these signals were necessary to convey certain information. Over time, the parents were better able to allow and encourage their daughter's expression of these signals. Validating the child's signals and learning how to respond to them appropriately eased the child's—and the parents'—distress. This little girl responded quite positively to treatment.

These ideas about signals and feelings also seem to work with so-called high-risk families, that is, families whose children are at significant risk of developing emotional disorders due to poverty, poor education, and lack of parental understanding of how to raise children. David Olds and his colleagues in Colorado have developed brilliant, successful early intervention and prevention strategies with a focus on understanding and regulating feelings. Similarly, Deborah Gross and her colleagues in Chicago studied young children who were at risk of developing conduct disorders and antisocial problems. They concluded that helping parents understand child development and feelings significantly decreased the number of children developing these problems when compared with families without such help.

Over time, then, I've seen the ideas about the signals and feelings work not just with patients and children at risk, but with children and parents in everyday real life. If you maximize your child's positive feelings—such as the signals for interest and enjoyment—and allow the child to express the signals for distress, anger, fear, and shame, and then you attend to the causes of those negative feelings, you'll have a happier, healthier child and parent.

The first part of this book looks at how children are born with the innate capacity to express their feelings using a preverbal communication system of nine signals. It also explores how the environment influences a child's feelings and expressions of those signals. Then the book asks you, as parent or other caregiver, to take time to examine yourself. You will have the chance to reflect on who you are emotionally and intellectually and to understand how you may influence the way your child develops.

The second part of the book explains each of the nine signals in detail and discusses ways in which parents and caregivers can respond wisely and appropriately to these signals.

It is my sense that all of us, all parents and caregivers—those who are at ease and those who are slightly bewildered, those who have already had three kids to learn from and those who are greeting their first child—can benefit from understanding the nine affects. And so do the children. The first twenty-four months of your child's life is a time when your baby's knowledge base is increasing by leaps and bounds, and it's a time when yours is too.

However, this book is about more than infancy. It focuses on the nine inborn signals, the embryology of emotional life, and the interaction with the environment during the preverbal years. Yet the nine affects and patterns explored here have relevance for you and your child far beyond your child's preverbal years—into toddlerhood, later childhood, adolescence, and adulthood. You may even find yourself understanding more about your own inner life and psychological dynamics. Parenthood is also a developmental stage in human life. You learn as you do, and the doing changes you and your child forever.

part
one

Understanding
Your Infant . . .
and Yourself

Welcome to Baby's World

[N]ature and nurture both play a role in all human behavior. Emotions are both the product of our evolution, particularly their physiology and expression, and of what we have learned, especially our attempts to manage our emotions, our attitudes about emotions and our representations of them verbally.

> —Paul Ekman, ed., in the Introduction
> to Charles Darwin's *The Expression of*
> *the Emotions in Man and Animals*

OTHER PEOPLE'S NEWBORN BABIES MAY SEEM LIKE PASSIVE, LITTLE loaves of bread—good smelling, nice to touch, but essentially just along for the ride. When you've got one of your own, however, you find out very quickly that they are intense, complex, vibrant little people. Even at their youngest, they gobble up sensory input and information from the outside world with enormous gusto.

Babies are social beings—not only do they need others to sustain their lives, they want and enjoy interaction with people. From their earliest days and weeks, they are sensing and then reacting to those around them. Granted, at first their outside world seems pretty small—a crib, a room, a breast, a pair of cradling arms—but that just makes the people who inhabit that tiny universe—mom and dad and other primary caregivers—all the more influential.

As parents of an infant, your mood, expressiveness, tone of voice, responsiveness, interest, and anxiety level all can have an impact on who your baby will become. Your child acquires communication skills and learns to express thoughts and feelings, to regulate tension and distress, and to feel confident or anxious, in large part through your behavior and your worldview. In so many ways, you influence your child's emerging personality and emotional character.

But your child doesn't simply absorb whatever you offer him, like a huge, thirsty sponge. He also "speaks up" and tells you what he needs, thinks, and feels. Every baby comes into this world with a lot of inborn characteristics and has a lot to say, even before he learns to talk.

How does he get his urgent messages across to you? Babies and parents set up a communication system right after birth. In place of words, a baby's vocabulary consists of nine signals that express his earliest emotions: *interest, enjoyment, surprise, distress, anger, fear, shame, disgust, and dissmell* (aversion to unpleasant odors). A halting cry, a wail, a scrunched-up face, a calm, sweet snuggle—these are the earliest means of self-expression.

Those first expressions modify and grow as quickly as an infant does. During the first weeks and months of your child's life, as you establish your relationship with each other, you will see that your little one is evolving into an independent personality with all the quirks and qualities that any one of us possesses as an adult. Watching this process of development is one of the delights—and challenges—of parenthood: The baby's first smile fills you with joy, but a child's anger or discontent may be bewildering and worrisome. Often, you may wonder just how your little baby came to be the person you hold in your arms.

Scientists and doctors, too, wonder about the complexity of a child's development. Some say that *nature* is primarily responsible for personality and behavior, that genetic programming and biochemical processes predetermine character. Others say *nurture* is most influential in shaping our character, that we are highly moldable by environment, circumstance, and interaction with people. Both, it turns out, are correct to some degree: Nature *and* nurture have an important impact, sometimes one more than the other. The newest studies from Daniel Stern and other infant researchers clearly show what observant moms and dads have known for thousands of years: How a child turns out is the result of a complex web of inborn attributes, the quality of the parents' caregiving, and the child's life circumstances and experiences.

What does all this mean to parents? I believe it means that they should focus on the interaction between nature and nurture, that is, how the *interaction between an infant and parent* influences a child's personality development. Why? Because interaction between parent and infant is what moms and dads have some control over—and it is what guides a child toward his or her emerging self-identity. As a parent, you can't do much about genetics or what goes on in the world at large, but you can do a lot about how you and your preverbal child interact and how that shapes your child's emotional development. Even though an enormous amount of emotional and intellectual development continues to take place after a child begins to talk, many habits of behavior and feeling can become ingrained in the early months of a child's life.

Fortunately, there has been an explosion of research into child development in recent years, and scientists have come to see how important the preverbal years can be to a child's healthy emotional development. They have begun to identify in more detail how the combination of a child's inherent nature and the child's experiences with parents and other environmental influences shapes a child's emerging personality.

What Nature Contributes:
The Influence of Genetics

As I've said, while every healthy child enters the world with the ability to express signals, each one has his or her own unique way of modulating those signals in reaction to what's going on in the outside world. This individual reactivity and expressiveness is what is generally called *temperament*. One of the more prominent theories about temperament suggests that children are born with a preset activity level—reflected in the amount of motion, and commotion, a child expresses. Other inherent traits may include:

- An internal body clock—governed by various biological functions, including the sleep cycle, eating patterns, digestive functions, and moods.
- Each child's approach to unknown circumstances— reflected in a child's degree of shyness or boldness.
- Adaptability to changes in routine—reflected in a child's flexibility and/or need for order.
- A child's overall mood—reflected in an infant's predisposition to be reflective, somber, laughing, shy, even depressive or aggressive.
- The ability to be persistent—reflected in an infant's threshold of frustration or patience.

- A child's sensory threshold—reflected in the level of sensitivity to sensory input such as colors or sound or flavors or light. Some children have extremely low tolerance for sound or are very bothered by lights; others seem not to be tuned in to flavors or to colors.
- The individual intensity of expression—reflected in a child's expression of the basic signals.
- The ease of distractibility when upset—reflected in a child's ability to control frustration, anxiety, anger, and impatience.

There is no doubt that inborn temperament exerts a real influence on a child's character, but I am convinced that very quickly experience influences children's emotional makeup. Some of their inherent emotional reflexes are accentuated, some diminished. It depends a lot on how the child experiences the world and how the world treats the child.

What Nurture Contributes: The Influence of Environment

Three important environmental forces shape a child's character. First, and most important, are parents and other caregivers. How a child's emotional character develops is directly influenced by the reception she receives from those who are responsible for her welfare. Throughout this book I hope to show how understanding the nine basic feelings provides the foundation for enhancing emotional development. For example, let's say a child who cannot tolerate loud noises is born into a household of quiet people who are fully committed to putting the needs of the child before their own whenever possible. They don't listen to much music or raise their voices often. It's just not their way. When their baby hears a loud crash on the street, she may cry, but chances are the parents recognize that the noise is startling and offer the child consolation and protection. That child will learn over time not to fear loud noises so much and will discover ways of handling unpleasant sounds. In time, loud noises may become less and less distressing.

On the other hand, a child who cannot tolerate loud noises may elicit anger from a parent who loves to play Beethoven's Fifth at concert volume—and isn't willing to put the baby's needs before his own. In this situation, when Dad turns up the CD player, baby howls. And if Dad can't control his anger over having his activity interrupted, then the child may not learn how to control her own reaction to the loud noise. In short, a parent who can't get a handle on his emotions might not be able to teach his child how to get a handle on hers. That's why whatever it is we are born with, how we emerge as an adult is also a product of the people and experiences we encounter from our first days in this world.

Culture also exerts an important influence on a child's development. The social mores and customs may influence the way inner feelings develop in children and how they are expressed. Culture changes how men and women think about themselves and their relationships to others and how groups of people experience self-worth and feel optimism. Racism, for example, can erode a sense of hope and of self-worth; in many societies, attitudes toward the role and nature of women can contribute to a young female's serious emotional struggles.

A third powerful influence is what I call unusual circumstances. Emotional or physical trauma, early loss of a parent, war, poverty, and violence exert enormous influence on how a child's emotions develop, although they do not have the same impact on each child. Violence can breed violence in some, or create depression and passivity in others. But difficult circumstances do not condemn children to a troubled life. Occasionally, for reasons we cannot completely explain, some children who endure terrible circumstances or events are able to bounce back and thrive. And for many others, therapeutic intervention, when needed, can help shape positive emotional development even in the face of dire distress and unfortunate events.

You are about to embark on an exciting journey of discovery as you and your baby live, love, and grow together. Every day will reveal to you your baby's emerging personality, and you will begin to see how it is formed through the combination of your child's own innate nature and the influence of your nurturing.

This book, I hope, will help you on this journey of discovery—about your child and about yourself as an individual and as a parent—so that your interactions with your child will bring you a lifetime of happiness and deep personal satisfaction.

I took a similar journey as a parent and as a doctor. And that journey has made me passionate about the importance of understanding and responding appropriately to a child's earliest expressions of emotion.

Interest

Enjoyment

Surprise

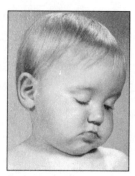

Distress

Anger

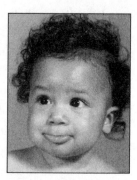

Fear

Shame

Disgust

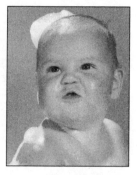

Dissmell

The Foundation of Feelings:
The Nine Basic Signals

Darwin proposed that there are certain innate discrete emotions that manifest themselves via distinct patterns of facial expression and postural muscle activity. . . . From Darwin's point of view, emotions are basically adaptive and help to organize behavior in ways that increase the chances of survival. . . . There is evidence that the basic innate emotions are present in the neonate and are fundamentally the same in infants across cultures.

—Taylor, Bagby, and Parker,
Disorders of Affect Regulation

Hallie is very expressive. Since she was three months old, whenever she's hungry she makes a little fake coughing sound, "Huh, huh," and then stares at me with a big open

11

*mouth. That's pretty expressive. And if she falls asleep
between us and then wakes up and is hungry again, she
kicks me to wake me up so I'll feed her. Now she's six
months old, and for the past couple of weeks, she's been
touching my breast when she wants some milk. If she's
upset, she scrunches her face and wails! This girl has powerful lungs. She's so much more interactive with me than I
expected. She really seems to be able to tell me what she is
feeling and needing.*

—Sheri, thirty-six, first-time mom

EXCITING RECENT RESEARCH SUGGESTS SOMETHING REMARKABLE:
Your baby arrives in this world with the ability to express feelings
and reactions using a preverbal language of nine innate signals.
These signals are expressed through a combination of facial
expressions, sounds, and body language. They communicate an
infant's responses to all kinds of stimuli, both internal, like a
painful gas bubble, and external, like a funny noise or an angry
voice. And they have been found in babies and adults of every culture studied so far.

*From day one, these signals are the child's language of need and
want.* And they are the basic foundation of an infant's complex
emotional character. They turn into feelings!

The nine signals can be grouped into two categories: *signals
of fun,* which include interest, enjoyment, and surprise; and *signals for help,* which include distress, anger, fear, shame, disgust
(an aversion to unpleasant tastes), and dissmell (an aversion to
unpleasant odors).

Interest and enjoyment are positive signals; surprise resets the nervous system in response to rapidly occurring stimulation; and distress, anger, fear, shame, disgust, and dissmell are negative signals. The fact that there are more negative than positive signals appears to be an evolutionary phenomenon: It is more important for the child's survival to be able to signal when it is in trouble than when it is not. (See Part Two of the book for more details on the individual signals.)

Understanding the Signals' Meanings

I remember when our son was born. Sometimes I felt that I was doing a good job of understanding his moods and expressions, but sometimes it was hard to know just what he was trying to tell us. As he got older, at times things seemed even more confusing and complex. But as I began learning more about these nine signals and about the emotions that develop from them, things seemed to fall into place.

You may experience much the same thing. When you bring your baby home from the hospital, you may learn, rather easily, that she's tired or hungry when she furrows her brow, lets out a plaintive cry, or frowns at you, with her mouth turned down. You'll see that enjoyment is expressed with a smile and a twinkle in the eye. But as your child grows, her feelings become more complicated—"I'm hungry" and "I'm tired" are no longer the two main messages. She'll begin to use signals to express everything from curiosity to disappointment, anger to love. And those may seem more difficult to decipher.

Well, luckily there is some solid research on how signals are expressed and what they mean. The human face—infant and adult—contains over twenty-five different muscles and is the main arena for exchange of these signals. Scientists using high-speed film, scans of the brain, and other methods have identified specific gestures, expressions, and sounds that are associated with each signal. Studies of infants document they will look at a human face above any other stimulus. And on that face, they will focus most on the area of the eyes, and next on the mouth. Infants are programmed to look for these facial expressions. Lively scientific controversy still exists over the exact number and nature of these built-in signals. For the purposes of this book the focus will be on the following nine.

- **Interest** is shown with the eyebrows slightly lowered or raised, concentrated looking and listening; the mouth may be a little open.

- **Enjoyment** elicits a smile, with the lips widened up and out.

- **Surprise** is associated with eyebrows up, eyes wide open and blinking, and the mouth in an "O" shape.

- **Distress** is revealed by crying, arched eyebrows, the corners of the mouth turned down, tears, and rhythmic sobbing.

- **Anger** is shown by a frown, eyes narrowed, a clenched jaw, and a red face.

- **Fear** is signaled by the eyes frozen open; skin pale, cold, and sweating; facial trembling, and hair erect.

- **Shame** is revealed by the lowering of the eyelids, and loss of muscle tone in the face and neck causing the head to hang down.

- **Disgust** elicits protruding lip and tongue.

- **Dissmell** causes the upper lip and nose to be raised and the head to be turned away.

Furthermore, each one of these signals operates on a continuum from low to high: interest to excitement; enjoyment to joy; surprise to startle; distress to anguish; anger to rage; fear to terror; and shame to humiliation. By watching your own child day in and day out, you will see how signals can escalate. For example, the signal for distress may mean "I'm tired and hungry." But simple hunger, expressed relatively mildly, may turn into anguish if you don't understand and respond reasonably promptly.

Not only do unattended signals often intensify, sometimes they change into other signals. For example: If interest and enjoyment are belittled or dismissed out of hand, they may trigger increasing feelings of shame. ("There must be something wrong with me if I'm enjoying what mom says is bad.") If distress intensifies, it turns into anguish; further intensification leads to anger.

Neurological studies have suggested that a child expresses one signal rather than another because the speed or quantity of different stimuli—such as hunger, a pretty balloon, or a loud noise—produce different patterns of neural firing and trigger different locations in the brain. For example, one hypothesis suggests any stimulus with a relatively sudden onset, such as a loud noise, will innately activate a surprise-to-startle response; if the stimulation does not have so sudden an onset, then fear is activated; and if the onset of the stimuli is still less rapid, then interest is elicited. In contrast, any stimulus that causes a sustained increase in the level of neural firing, such as a continuing loud noise, automatically activates a cry of distress; if the noise is sustained and even louder, it activates the anger response; and, conversely, any sudden decrease in stimulation would innately activate the smile of enjoyment (Figures 1–3 in the Charts appendix illustrate these patterns).

The affects of shame, disgust, and dissmell operate a bit differently. Babies may tend to express shame somewhat later than the other signals. Shame involves the absence of a confirming, validating response. Shame operates only after the signals of interest and/or enjoyment have been activated—and it acts to interfere with one or the other or both. In addition, shame, shyness, guilt, and discouragement may have an identical core, although later the child experiences them somewhat differently. Shame is about inferiority; shyness is about strangeness of the other; guilt is about moral transgression; and discouragement is about temporary defeat. Shame also appears intimately related to self-esteem. Many child development researchers suggest that the development of a healthy sense of self and self-esteem involves validation of the positive affects of interest and enjoyment and a growing sense of competency. Because the inappropriate and excessive use of shame hampers the signals for interest and enjoyment, shame erodes self-esteem.

Disgust and dissmell are considered to be survival responses designed to protect a child from harmful foods and odors. Disgust is related to taste and the gastrointestinal system; nausea and vomiting can help rid the body of dangerous substances. Dissmell involves the olfactory system, with the typical evasive maneuvers visible in infancy. The early warning response via the nose is dissmell; the next level of response, from the mouth or stomach, is disgust. Later, these signals are related psychologically to rejection and contempt. Such phrases as "this leaves a bad taste in my mouth" or "this has a bad smell to it" convey the link between the physiological affects of disgust/dissmell and psychological rejection and contempt.

It is also important to note that these nine signals don't operate in a vacuum. They can trigger other signals and may interact with one another. For example, excessive distress, fear, or shame may trigger anger; and interruption of interest may lead to distress and then anger.

Responding to Your Infant's Signals:

The Five Keys

We [emphasize] the role of early relationships in affect development and in the acquisition of affect-regulating capacities. These are complex developmental processes, however, that are influenced by other factors as well, including temperament and neurobiological structures and functions, and the reciprocal interactions between these endowments and the early social environment.

—Taylor, Bagby, and Parker,
Disorders of Affect Regulation

When the infant's caretakers act to soothe and hold it, the infant internalizes the qualities and functioning of its caretaking environment. This will have an effect on how the

19

infant perceives and experiences danger, tolerates affects, and develops a capacity to allay its own anxieties.

—Ivri Kumin, *Pre-Object Relatedness*

You ask about crying—Jessie cried a lot. Sometimes it seemed nonstop. In the old days they would have said she had colic, now they attribute it to all kinds of problems with allergies, foods, exposure to smoke. She cried so much that it was impossible to know what she wanted or needed. It wasn't until she was several months old that it stopped. By then both she and I were worn out. I have three other kids, eight, four, and two, and it's been tough sometimes. With Jessie, who is six months old now, I have to make a special effort to pay attention when she cries or fusses. My inclination was to ignore it a little bit. But now that's she's getting bigger she can be consoled, I can actually do some good for her. I just have to learn not to shut down when she starts to crank up the volume. I have to remember she is sending me a message and I need to try to figure out what it is. Is she tired? Hungry? Sick? Anxious? Usually these days, I figure it out. And sometimes my other kids are a real big help in identifying the cause.

—Marie, forty, mother of four

ALTHOUGH THE SECOND HALF OF THE BOOK DEALS IN MORE DETAIL with each of the nine signals, I want to take some time here to talk about the process of learning to understand their meanings and responding to them. Becoming comfortable with your child's expressions of the signals can provide enormous benefits to both of you: It helps the two of you establish a good relationship; it helps your child develop the ability to regulate tension and increases the feelings of happiness and security; and it can prevent all kinds of problems and enhance your child's potential.

The actual process of perceiving and responding to your infant's signals requires you to be aware that the infant has these signals and he is making an effort to communicate. Next, it requires you to internally integrate your baby's incoming message with your own understanding, past experience, and so on, so you can sort out the possible meaning of the signal—that is, the meaning of the message that's being sent. And, finally, the process includes a response from the adult. Dr. Ivri Kumin, a psychoanalyst in Seattle, Washington, has recently written an elegant book called *Pre-Object Relatedness* that delves into these processes in great detail.

Listen, Understand, and Respond

You already may have had this sort of experience: Baby starts fussing while you are doing the laundry, talking on the phone, getting dinner, or taking a shower. On any given day, you may react differently—depending on your own mood, your degree of alertness to what's going on, outside pressures, or just plain old exhaustion. But let's say you finally call out, "Hey, sweetie, I'm talking to Grandma. I'll be there in a minute." The baby quiets down after she's heard your voice and you go back to the call. It's not a solution, however. Pretty soon the baby starts up again, more persistently and louder. You figure she is just unhappy because she isn't the center of your attention right now and she can learn to live with it another minute or so. You don't call out this time, instead you walk with the phone into another room to try to hear over the crying. Suddenly, baby launches into full-scale, air-gasping bawling. You're irritated and the baby's angry. You hang up and rush to see what's going on. Now it's not easy to get her to calm down. You feel miffed and frustrated. And so does baby. You try a bottle; check her diaper; walk her around the room; show her the stuffed animals. You work to figure out what signals the baby was sending and why. And often there's no one to pat you on the back or bring you a cup of tea or say sweet things in your ear. You've got to calm yourself down.

All this happened simply because when baby signaled "Hey! I'm over here. Where are you?" you ignored the question and tried to pretend that nothing was being said to you. Imagine if it had been your friend or partner calling out. If you simply ignored them instead of responding appropriately, they'd get ticked off and feel dismissed. Same with baby.

That's why, even when it seems like you can never have a moment for yourself, and it all feels like too much, you and baby will end up less hassled and more attuned to one another if you respond appropriately. You might say to the person on the other end of the phone, "I have to go check the baby for a minute. Hold on." Then, if you need to change the diaper, or pick baby up, you tell your caller, "I gotta scoot. Call you back when I can." It may seem frustrating not to finish your call, but you can bet your life will be a whole lot less frustrating if you attend to baby in a timely fashion.

That said, I don't mean that you can never, ever respond slowly to your child's signals. There's little harm from an occasional miscommunication or the inevitable frustration that results—after all, there is a lot going on in your life at any given moment. The trick is not to respond so slowly that the baby is traumatized. Every child and adult is going to experience frustration at some time; it is part of life and learning how to handle it is necessary for sound emotional development. So you don't need to be overly anxious and rush to decrease the slightest frustration or deny the child a chance to overcome it on his own. If, however, you establish a pattern of inattention or permit traumatizing levels of frustration, you are going to produce longer-term negative repercussions. Remember, while babies are often resilient, they can be quite delicate when it comes to their emerging feelings. Single episodes of misunderstanding rarely cause lasting damage, but repeated misunderstanding of signals can cause problems. If your child finds that you regularly miss, ignore, or respond unhelpfully to her signals, she will have a far harder time developing a positive sense of self and will have a difficult time feeling she can depend on you. In addition, spending time with your infant and child sends the message that she is interesting and loved and enhances her internal sense of being valued and important.

Five Keys to Raising a Happy, Capable, Responsible Child

Throughout this book, I often mention five key issues in child development that have emerged from recent scientific studies. The first four involve the signals directly and provide a simple outline of how a wise parent can best communicate with an infant; the fifth involves the parent-child relationship specifically. They are: (1) encouraging the reasonable expression of all signals, positive and negative; (2) maximizing the signals of fun—interest and enjoyment; (3) attending to the signals for help and dealing with whatever triggers them; (4) putting words to the signals as soon as possible and labeling the feelings. The fifth key is to be aware of your child's intense desire to be like you.

Let's look at each of these points in some detail.

Key #1—Allow Full, Reasonable Expression of All Signals

Allowing and encouraging the expression of signals of fun and signals for help is perhaps the most important key to establishing good communication with your child and nurturing healthy emotional development.

Signals for fun—interest and enjoyment—are positive signals. If you and your child can discover what he is interested in, and you both believe that his interests are important, your baby has a better chance to understand himself and his potential, and ultimately to find a fulfilling life's focus to which he can give 110 percent.

You can encourage and reinforce these positive signals by observing and validating what stimulates your child's interest/ enjoyment and finding opportunities to offer her other similar activities and experiences throughout the day. For example, when handing your child her much-loved stuffed toy, you might say, "What a wonderful teddy bear you have." At the playground, you can reinforce her delight by saying, "What fun it is to swing. Wheee!" If you see that she has been looking at a book, then you can make sure the two of you take time to read together before she goes to bed.

Signals for help—distress, anger, fear, shame, disgust, and dissmell—are negative signals. Encouraging their expression allows the baby to ask for and receive assistance when she needs it. This process of expression and response validates a child's inner feelings and helps her learn how to manage distress and tension. One of the first positive messages you can transmit to your child is that she has entered a world in which it is safe to express both positive and negative emotions.

Sometimes, parents try to help their children overcome distress by telling them to "Buck up!" or "Have a stiff upper lip." This can be unhelpful. For example, if Susie becomes frightened and cries out when a dog approaches and her dad says, "Don't be a crybaby," or "That dog isn't going to hurt you," he is telling her that what she feels is not valid. Susie feels very strongly that there is a good reason to be distressed—the dog looks huge and unpredictable. If her dad dismisses the feeling, Susie will question her perception, her rightness in feeling what she believes to be a realistic assessment of her situation, and that in turn may erode her self-confidence and self-esteem. In addition, by dismissing her signal of distress, Dad is telling Susie that he is not going to protect her even when she directly asks. Susie's signal for fear is, after all, her only way of asking for immediate help. By denying that assistance, Dad undermines his daughter's sense of security and trust in him.

Even when a signal may need to be redirected, as when your child's signal for interest is being expressed by pulling a dog's ear, you should acknowledge and encourage it. "That's a beautiful dog, isn't it" you might say as you gently remove your child's hand from the dog. "We need to learn to pet him softly." Or, for example, your child may express the signal for interest by throwing pots and pans out of the cupboards. If that's not to your liking, the best solution is not to discourage the interest, but to give the child's interest another outlet. Substitute another toy for the clanging pans or place some toys in a paper bag so the child can get them out of there, instead of removing things from the cupboard.

Suppressing the expression of a signal, whether positive or negative, is not the way to cultivate a healthy, well-controlled child. Children who are not encouraged to express their interest in and enjoyment of the world can turn out to have their potential and capacities constricted. Children who are made to bottle up their negative signals for help can develop escalating feelings of being misunderstood, rage, sullenness, withdrawal, and/or depression.

In technical terms, Key #1 can be stated briefly as: minimize affect inhibition.

Key #2—Maximize Signals of Interest and Enjoyment

Not only do you want to allow your child to express a full range of emotions using the signals, you want especially to maximize the signals for interest and enjoyment. You can do this by noticing what your child enjoys—books, animals, pots and pans—and looking for opportunities to repeat those enjoyable activities. And even if you think that what she enjoys is disruptive, don't squash it. If you need to moderate her interest, do so in a way that tells your child that you enjoy the fact that she is interested and having a good time. For example, say your child grabs a book or magazine and begins to tear the pages. If the book or magazine is not precious, take a moment to observe how the sound, the feel, the smell of the pages, and the action of tearing is intriguing to your child; or ask yourself if she may be imitating Dad's tearing something out of the newspaper. Then, let your child know you recognize and appreciate her interest: "That's a wonderful magazine, isn't it? Such nice pictures, and such great paper." If you want to take it away from your child so it stays in one piece, offer another piece of paper in its place and say, "That magazine is not for tearing up, but here's a nice piece of paper that you can play with all you want." I recall one mother who found her young son putting Cheerios in a book, mashing them, and then delightedly opening the book and watching the powder fall out. Her initial reaction? "Oh my gosh! What are you doing? What a mess!" The little boy's lower lip started quivering, and his eyes filled with tears. Then his mother "got it"! "Oh, this is really neat, isn't it? What a great sound . . . and a cool result! Pulverizing those Cheerios. Do you want to do this some more? Okay . . . let's use this old book, get these Cheerios, take your shoes off, and we'll put you some place that's easy to clean up . . . the bathtub? Out on the porch?" The little boy had a blast, and it gave the mother a good opportunity, if she had the time and inclination, to teach a little physics: use of force, changes from one form of a substance to another, and so on. In addition, such activity may have some psychological meaning of importance to the child. In other words, something about the "play" may be related to certain feelings or wanting to be like mother (a pharmacist) or father (a chemist).

Or perhaps your child dumps a boxful of paper clips on the floor. Rather than simply grabbing them from her hands and chastising her for making a mess, you can set limits and establish rules and still let your child know you appreciate her impulse to explore and to be interested in what she sees. Take the time to say, "Hey, what have you discovered here? These are paper clips. Aren't they funny looking. Here, let me show you how to put them back in the box. You know, they are too small for you to play with. You might swallow them. Let's put them back and play with your toy here instead." This allows you to protect your child, while letting her know that you are tuned in to her way of seeing the world and are interested in helping her discover and understand new things. The youngest child will understand the import of what you are saying, even if she can't comprehend the exact meaning of the words. And don't worry if what she is interested in—a stick, a potholder, a scrap of paper, a piece of fuzz—makes no sense to you. It has caught her interest and that is all you need to know.

Technically, Key #2 is stated as: maximize positive affects.

Key #3—Remove Triggers for Distress

In addition to maximizing your child's positive signals of interest and enjoyment, you also want to act appropriately when your child sends out signals of distress. Your child depends on you for protection. When something is upsetting, first you acknowledge the validity of your child's feeling and express your sympathy. But then you want to remove the cause of the distress, and reduce your child's anxiety. Early on, infants and young children signal distress primarily because they are hungry, tired, sick, in pain, or need their diapers changed. When a baby cries because her diapers are wet, it's a simple matter of changing them promptly. Other situations may be more difficult to negotiate. Say your child has taken to crying whenever someone wearing glasses comes into view. You may feel upset or embarrassed at the child's reaction. You may try to ignore the situation or dismiss the upset. This will only tell the child that you do not understand and will invalidate your child's signal of distress. Then the upset can escalate. Actually, glasses can distort a person's face and eyes, and such distortions can be very disruptive to infants and small children who are so tuned in to facial expressions as a built-in way of communicating. Perhaps, instead, you can pick up the child and turn her away from the person. You also might ask that person to take his glasses off, or ask if your child can examine them.

The technical phrase for Key #3 is: minimize negative affects (causes, not expressions).

Key #4—Use Words, Even with Newborns, to Express Signals

Before kids can understand everything you say to them, your words, tone of voice, gestures, and expression all help make your meaning clear. By talking to your child, you are acknowledging her presence as a separate individual—an important step in building the child's sense of self. In addition, by labeling situations and signals you are showing your child how to use *words as a substitute for overt actions.* Eventually, she will see that there's no need to yell incoherently when she can more accurately communicate what she's thinking and feeling with a few well-chosen words. In fact, when caretakers put words to feelings for an infant, it actually helps the young brain develop more ways to process information and emotions. It expands preverbal communications to include verbal expression. And you lay the foundation for good tension regulation when you teach your child to identify feelings and find ways to express them verbally. When children are adept at an early age at expressing their emotions verbally, they are able to avoid a lot of childhood frustrations because they are able to negotiate for their interests and needs.

You can help make your child comfortable with using words to express emotions by *labeling the signals* as they are expressed. For example, when your infant cries because she is hungry, don't just feed her, take the time to talk to her, too. You might want to say: "I hear you, little one. Are you hungry now? Let's get you something to eat." When your baby is startled by a car horn, you might say, "That was a terrible noise. It really startled you." When your child is enjoying the swings, you might use words to reinforce the positive experience. You can make emphatic sounds like "Wheee!" or say "You are having fun, aren't you." This not only validates the child's feelings, but puts words to various physical sensations.

You can give your child a wide range of words to use for all kinds of feelings: happy, silly, snippy, angry, grumpy, exuberant, ecstatic, meltdown, tired. If you use such words to identify moods and emotions, they will eventually find their way into the child's speech when she learns to talk. One mom, who was very good about labeling her son's emerging feelings, told me this story: "When Steven was in preschool, around five years old, he had a teacher who was sometimes moody. We worried that she was kind of hard on the kids and eventually we did move him to another class. Prior to that, I must say he coped pretty well. One day he came home and said, 'Mom, you wouldn't believe it— Mrs. Henderson was so snippy today!' I know that being able to express his perception of her mood helped him cope. He didn't feel so victimized."

Key #5—Be Aware of Your Child's Desire to Be Like You

Infants and young children are eager to be like Mom and Dad. To your child, you are the universe—the force that shapes his emerging sense of self and teaches him how to behave. Extensive research has shown how powerful these early patterns of identification are. When it comes to helping your child learn tension regulation and rules of conduct, identification is your most powerful tool. (For more information see Chapter 7.)

Think about it. If your two-year-old lets out a "Damn!" when he falls down, he has probably heard Mom or Dad say that word in similar situations. Even before they can speak, kids absorb those kinds of messages—and many more that are far less obvious. If you react to your child's signals for anger by becoming agitated and angry yourself, your child will think that's the appropriate response. She'll learn that anger calls for more anger. The result? A child who just gets more and more wound up as emotions intensify.

Parents who are calm and comfortable with a full range of their own emotions teach their children to be well modulated emotionally as well. Consider this scene: Sonia, a one-year-old, tottered over to look behind the TV at all the fascinating wires and plugs. Her father spotted her and said quietly, "Sonia, those wires can hurt you if they are plugged in. Electricity goes through them. Here, let me show you how it works with this extension cord that is not plugged in. Or we can play with this neat ball." Sonia turned away from the wires and went to her Dad, who explained a bit more about wires and electricity using the unplugged extension cord. Then she happily went to play with the ball. "Thank you for not playing with those wires, Sonia. I love you," said her dad. Sonia's father intervened in a number of ways: He talked with his daughter in a calm voice, telling her the wires were dangerous. Even though she couldn't understand all the words, she understood the meaning and the tone of voice. In addition, she was exposed to the important process of using words instead of actions to express ideas and feelings. Dad was urgent—but instead of sweeping down and shouting, he calmly communicated the feelings with words. He also offered Sonia an alternate source of stimulation—the ball. Finally, he used positive reinforcement ("Thank you. I love you.") to elicit and reward a change in behavior. This is much more effective than negative reinforcement or punishment. All of the father's actions and reactions are teaching Sonia valuable information lessons that will help her grow up into an adult who is kind, calm and in tune with her feelings.

More Ways to Handle Signals

When it comes to responding appropriately to your infant's signals, every parent can use a couple of shortcuts. Here are some time-tested ways to make it easier to get along together, even when you are reaching the end of your rope.

Try Distraction. If you want your infant or young child to stop what he is doing, provide an equally intriguing alternative. Don't want the newspaper shredded on the floor (and then eaten)? Offer a book (one of the indestructible kid's books now on the market), or change the venue completely by bringing out a favorite toy, or by walking with your child into another room.

Provide Choices. If you want your child to dress warmly, give her a choice between a warm coat or a couple of layers of warm shirts. This lets her feel she has some control and independence and helps her develop her taste. But don't offer too many choices—that can breed chaos and indecision. The goal is to find the workable balance.

Use Rewards, Not Punishment, Whenever Possible. Teaching a child how to behave can be a positive experience for child and parent; it's fun for you to help your child grow and your child will feel a great deal of pride and happiness when she does things "right" and is able to win your praise.

Whenever your child responds to instruction as you wish, offer thanks and tell her how proud you are of what she's done. "That's great! Thanks for putting the knife back down on the table." "See how much better it looks when we pick your books up off the floor? Thanks for helping me put them on the table." These simple expressions of your approval will do far more to make sure your child learns the lessons you are trying to impart than any amount of punishment.

As your understanding of the meaning and purpose of the nine signals grows, you may find your ideas about punishment evolving. This will be discussed in more detail in chapter 20. But I want to emphasize here that if you use criticism or hitting (spanking) to influence behavior, it is probably because you feel you have run out of alternatives. Take time to come up with other ways of managing conflicts. And remember, in the short run motivating by fear and shame may work, but in the long run it comes at great cost to your child and to your relationship.

Swat your child's hand for picking up the knife and she doesn't learn what knives are or what to do with the knife (put it back on the table or don't pick it up in the first place). What she learns is that if she expresses interest in something you don't like, you'll make her feel bad. That can either make her hesitant to express her own interests (which can put a real damper on learning and happiness) or simply teach her that she is a lot better off doing the things she enjoys far out of your reach. Spend a decade or more reinforcing that message and you've got a pretty alienated teenager.

Constant criticism—even if it isn't followed up with punishment—also erodes self-confidence. Many children are tenderhearted. They are easily crushed by feelings of failure or shame when they are told over and over that they don't measure up to a parent's expectations. When you are unhappy with something your child is doing, try enforcing rules by example and teaching self-control by being controlled yourself.

What About Spoiling the Baby?

Some parents worry that if a child is allowed to be too enthusiastic or to express anger he will become spoiled. I want to state emphatically that anything you can ever do to elicit a smile, enthusiasm, or joy in a child, do it! And anything you can do to let your child know that feelings of anger or unhappiness are valid and deserve to be attended to quickly, do it!

Soon enough, life will provide more than an ample supply of frustration and heartache. Parents don't need to—and shouldn't—supply such troubles. It's simply mean to say to a child, "You are going to have to learn this lesson, kiddo. Life isn't nice and it's often tough." For children, learning about life's hard knocks— instead of being protected from them—is no favor. Strong, buoyant, optimistic children emerge from families where parents protect them from unhappiness and frustration while encouraging expression of feelings. True strength comes from competence and a reasonably positive sense of self—two qualities that thrive when children are allowed to express a full range of emotions at the same time they are guided toward positive feelings.

A New Way of Thinking About Control: Helping Your Child Develop Tension Regulation

Allowing your child a full range of expression of the nine signals does not mean that you have given up control. In fact, this process actually allows you to take charge of both your parenting role and your child's healthy emotional development.

You can guide your child toward the behavior you want and still handle the signals wisely. At one time or another, for example, every parent has to interrupt a child's signals of excitement or anger. While you want to allow your child *reasonable* expression of feelings, you need to step in when your child needs help cooling down. Uncontrolled outbursts, marked by kicking, biting, or throwing things, may be important signals of distress or anger. But if they are ongoing, they may require containment and holding as well as verbal labeling. You want to help teach tension regulation—that is, the ability to modulate feelings and manage emotional ups and downs both internally and when interacting with people—not tension excess. So if your child becomes too wound up, try using phrases such as, "That new toy sure is exciting, isn't it?" "That's neat—you really are excited!" "You really were frightened by that loud noise, weren't you? Let's cuddle here for a minute until you feel better." "I'm so sorry you got hurt; how distressing! Do you feel better now?" These are comforting phrases that take the emotions down a notch and teach your child how to regulate his own feelings. Sometimes, you may have to hold the child or carry him from the room. But the wise management of specific situations will not dampen your child's emotional growth.

On the other hand, the use of shame or suppression of feel-

Help your child and yourself—put water on the fire, not gasoline!

ings does not help your child learn how to self-regulate his own intense feelings. "Stop jumping around—calm down! You look so silly!" "Don't be a crybaby—it didn't hurt that much. Try to control yourself!" If you say these kinds of things as your infant becomes increasingly agitated, you only increase the child's distress. The child will have a hard time learning how to calm down.

Tension regulation, once learned, allows your child to

become comfortable with the feeling and expression of a wide range of emotions and to develop self-assurance. It also allows your child to develop the ability to be self-soothing. He learns how to depend on himself—not you—to calm down after experiencing excessive frustration, distress, or anger.

Some parents, however, have a hard time teaching their children to become self-soothing, particularly if they feel that a child should learn through experiencing conflict and discomfort. It is hard for them to accept that the smart technique is to *pour water, not gasoline, on a fire.* Or, as Goethe succinctly stated: "Less heat, more light!"

One woman and her young daughter, Maria, showed me how this can be a problem. Maria often became distressed when there were a lot of other kids around. All her mother had to do was take her child to the side and read to her for a couple of minutes, but she refused to use the technique. "I think my daughter should have to learn to deal with people," she told me. "It won't do her any good if I take her out of the situation every time she gets a little bit upset. How is she ever going to learn to cope?" It took me a long time to help this mother understand that by allowing Maria to spin out of control and get superdistressed, she was actually making it harder for her child to learn to deal with other people. I suggested to her that if she would help her daughter cool off, then the little girl could find more satisfactory ways, more quickly, to get along in potentially distressing situations. Maria could then internalize this kind of cooling-off process and soothe herself.

Other parents have a hard time helping their children develop tension regulation because they themselves have never learned to modulate their frustrations. They have difficulty expressing intense emotions without going to extremes. Since kids are such eager imitators of their parents' behavior, a mom or dad without good self-control will pass on patterns of unregulated emotional response to the child. This may create a cycle of unhappiness. In many instances, adults with poor tension regulation may be self-destructive and/or violent toward others. In addition, alcohol and drug abuse, domestic abuse, antisocial behavior, or having troubled relationships may all result from impaired tension regulation.

On the other hand, a child who has good tension regulation is happier, calmer, and more socially comfortable as she grows up. She is able to form a solid sense of who she is and what she wants so that as an adult she can cope with the often overwhelming stresses and tensions of daily life. She becomes comfortable with and understanding of her feelings.

Another significant benefit of learning to respond appropriately to the signals is that doing so builds a child's self-esteem. Every time you acknowledge and validate a child's expression of feeling, you tell the child that his perceptions are accurate and deserving of attention. Over time this produces in a child a sense of confidence and the ability to know what he feels and wants and to stick up for it.

Responding to Signals As Your Child Grows:

Watching the Vocabulary Become More Complex

Being able to share emotions is extremely important for [emotional] development, because it is the sharing of emotions with the infant that [tells the child his feeling] is understood.

> —Joy Osofsky, "Affective develop-
> ment and early relationships:
> Clinical implications"

I'll never forget the first time that Charlie told me he was mad at me—I mean told me in no uncertain terms. We had been driving in the car for about an hour and he was in the

car seat. He'd been quiet for a while but all of a sudden he
started making a lot of sounds and gestures. He was in the
backseat and I couldn't really see him except in the rearview
mirror. Traffic was heavy. I didn't pay much attention, just
muttered a few words at him. Finally, he let loose and threw
a toy at the back of my head. Then he started making sounds
that, without words, still sounded exactly like my wife when
she gets mad at me. The rhythm, the inflection, the harsh
tone. I didn't know whether to laugh, cry, or scream at him.
I had to pull the car over and get composed. I thought, "My
God, he's got a lot more to get off his chest than I thought!"

—Sam, forty-two, father of a two-
year-old and a fourteen-year-old

THE NINE INBORN SIGNALS DO NOT DISAPPEAR WITH GROWTH;
they are with us for life. An eight-month-old baby has the same
nine signals as a fourteen-month-old. What changes is that the
nine signals become refined and interlinked as they are shaped by
life experience. For example, as a child grows and experiences
instances of loss, the signal for distress can be expanded to
include sadness; or various experiences may make a child express
a blend of disgust and anger as contempt.

With each new day your child is acquiring an ever more complex
set of tools for expressing herself and reacting to the world at large. It
is helpful if you understand what you can and cannot expect from an
infant at different ages, so that you are able to accept how she
expresses her feelings and needs. Here's how the current under-

standing of infant development ties into and underscores the basic principles we have outlined about handling signals.

The Child's First Eighteen Months: A Growing Sense of Self

During the first eighteen months of an infant's life there is a lot going on—in the brain, the body, the emotions, the personality, and the ego structure. At different ages, a child has different capacities: a four-week-old does not have the physical ability to move around independently or a clear sense of himself as differentiated from others; a fourteen-month-old can run from room to room and knows perfectly well how to strategize to win your attention or rile you up. Both kids are using the same signals of interest or distress, for example, but they are able to play them out in differing ways.

The insights into child development laid out in this section are based in large part on the work of Daniel Stern, M.D., who has spent his career looking into the mind and heart of the infant. Stern is a psychoanalyst and infant researcher, currently affiliated with Brown University. He is the author of several interesting books, including *The Interpersonal World of the Infant: A View from Psychoanalysis and Developmental Psychology* and *The Diary of a Baby*, a description of what goes on in the mind of an infant.

Birth to Two Months

During the first two months of life, a child's focus is on some pretty basic activities—regulating and stabilizing the sleep–awake, day–night, and hunger–satiation cycles. This is important work physically and emotionally. Establishing these essential life patterns, with the help of Mom and Dad, allows an infant to become oriented to the overwhelming new world. Children this age are a bundle of highly reactive impulses, and the interactions between parent and child and all the new information flooding his brain—from sleeping, waking, eating, and bathing to diaper changing—establish the first building blocks for a child's emerging sense of self.

During this time a child is sending out signals of interest, distress, and so on. And even this early in life, a child is using the feedback she gets to begin to assemble a picture of the world at large and her place in it.

Parents are important companions in the process. Researchers have found that during these first weeks of life children are programmed to expect that their parents will relate to them in a cyclic pattern of attention and nonattention that takes a few minutes to complete. When the cycle is interrupted—a child is not given attention for too long a time—he can become agitated. A child needs to be constantly, if intermittently, the focus of your attention. Research also shows that a child's main focus is on the parents' eyes and mouth. This highlights how the child is already zeroing in on the parents' signals, which, like baby's, are communicated through facial expressions centering around the eyes and mouth.

All this back-and-forth has profound effects on the child's brain: sights, sounds, smells, and touch help build new neural connections, shaping the way the mind will function emotionally and intellectually. Early, repeated physical, emotional, and intellectual experiences affect the way a child's brain is wired. A child who is abandoned or emotionally neglected very early in life may never fully develop a sense of attachment or empathy. A child who is spoken to a great deal during his first two years, and is encouraged to respond, is more likely to have good language skills later on.

Two Months to Seven to Nine Months

In the first two months, give and take may seem pretty one sided—the parent gives, the baby takes—but from the start there is a lot of interaction going on. At about two to three months infants become aware that there are other people out there who are separate and different from themselves. They also begin to have a sense of time—past and present—and their position in it.

Between two and seven months, the child becomes even more interactive—both giving and taking. She is becoming aware of herself, her impact on others, and their responses to her. This emerging sense of identity is formed by a growing awareness of her own personal desires and her ability to express those desires.

During this period, infants also begin to put together a picture of how their senses of touch, sight, taste, hearing, and smell interrelate and how they are used to make sense of the world at large. For example, infants this age quickly learn to associate motion—being picked up by mom—with sound—mom saying, "Uuup goes the baby," drawing out the "up," matching the physical feeling of lifting with the mother's voice. They become aware that meaning can be conveyed through various modes of expression. And they learn that each sense can produce a whole range of sensations: hearing music may be exciting, soothing, or even scary.

At this point, a child's signals are beginning to be used for "conversations." A parent's response should be to follow the same guidelines that apply to any satisfactory conversation: You listen, you don't interrupt, you are interested in what the other person has to say, you offer appropriate feedback, and you express your feelings or ideas in exchange. In other words, when the baby laughs with delight when she sees a favorite stuffed animal, you laugh too and say, "Isn't that a fun teddy? You like Teddy, don't you?" And then you hand her the teddy bear and perhaps make a funny noise. In response, your child may make a series of gurgling noises and smile or wave her arms. That's more "talk." You then respond in kind and you both laugh together. You two are having a conversation, as glorious as the most adult exchange, packed full of information.

In your child's brain, the network of connections is growing increasingly complex: Over time, the child's brain will establish millions and millions of neural connections, and then as it matures it will eliminate the ones that are not used or needed. This is the physical consolidation of knowledge and of emotional and behavioral patterns.

Seven to Nine Months to Fifteen to Eighteen Months

During these months kids become much more expressive and interactive. They begin to realize that one person can understand the feelings of another and they want to share what they see, feel, and think. At this age, when a child transmits a signal, he is seeking active confirmation that the world hears him loud and clear and that it is concerned not just with his behavior (eating, crying, going outside) but with the quality of his deep feelings. If a child this age is neglected, he may begin to develop a sense of isolation and despair that he will ever be understood.

Parents can tune in to the child's need at this time pretty easily. For example, I once observed this scene: Josh, an eight-and-a-half-month-old boy, was reaching for a toy just out of his reach. As he tensed his body to squeeze out the needed extra inch of reach he made a grunting noise. At that moment, his mother joined in, saying "Uuuuuh . . . uuuuuh!" Josh's look of frustration dissolved and he looked at Mom happily as she picked him up just enough so that he could reach the toy. Mom's mimicking of Josh's efforts was perfectly in tune with his experience: She was expressing effort and acknowledging a bit of his frustration, too.

But what if that had not happened? Imagine that as Josh was struggling for that toy just out of reach, his mom ignored his efforts. His distress might increase to the point that he would let out a howl and start crying. And that could lead to a conflict between mom and son. Now suppose that this sort of disregard and escalation of distress was repeated over and over in many sit-uations. Pretty soon Josh would start believing that his feelings were somehow unacceptable and even shameful.

Here's another example of how, at this age, parents' reactions to signals may be helpful or hurtful to their child. Recently, I was on a playground and observed a bright, active, smiling infant named John crawling around in the sandbox with others kids. At one point he tumbled off the edge of the sandbox and landed facedown in the sand. He started wailing. A young man who happened to be right there patted him on the back, helped him sit up, and said: "Are you all right? That was quite a tumble!" His mother came over at that point, and John looked up at her, crying.

The young man said: "He took quite a fall."

She said to John, in a tone that was not harsh but not com-forting either: "You're not hurt. You're okay. You don't need to cry."

John started crying harder, and his mother picked him up and said: "That didn't hurt. You're okay." He continued to cry, and she said: "If you keep on crying, we're just going to have to leave." With that, he began howling, his face red and contorted.

"Okay," she said, "with you crying like this we're going to have to leave." And off she went, holding a wailing John in her arms.

What happened here? Perhaps saying "You're not hurt" and "That didn't hurt" were her attempts to comfort and to reassure herself; or perhaps she was embarrassed by John's crying, as if it conveyed a lack of vigilance on her part; or perhaps she was of the school that believes males shouldn't show their feelings. But whatever her motives, the result was that she was not attuned to her son's feelings and was disregarding his signals for help. And that only made him more upset and her more impatient.

This kind of "You're not hurt," or "Be brave," or "You're too sensitive" type of response—the dismissal of the child's feelings and experience—can be very disruptive no matter what age the child. It will send a toddler into a tantrum and a teenager out the door. Such a response completely disregards the child's true feelings of being scared and or hurt. It tells the child that his feelings are just plain wrong—when they are neither right nor wrong, they simply *are* and deserve recognition. Mom missed an opportunity to become closer, to get in tune, with the child.

A more productive response would be first to kiss the boo-boo. Giving kisses makes your child feel you care about him; the kiss also tells him you understand the hurt and share his feelings. And then you might tell the child that you know the tumble was scary. You might even try saying, "I know you were distressed and maybe even a little angry because I didn't protect you." Your response might sound stilted, but it is important because it increases your awareness of how your child feels, validates the child's signal, and starts his process of labeling feelings, which is vital if he is to learn to use words to manage emotions. This is also important because your use of consolation, validation, and labeling can lead to hopefulness and optimism in the child.

This kind of attunement between parent and child has one more important benefit: It allows the child to develop a sense of empathy and caring for others, abilities that are essential if he is to have a full and satisfying life.

In some instances, a child may seem to be overreacting or playing to the crowd, but that is usually because he needs caring and emotional attention he is not getting. If your child exhibits this behavior, it is worth asking yourself if that may be the case. I remember a little boy who, when playing soccer at a very young age, would become distressed and tearful over every minor collision or play. Is it any surprise that his parents were of the "You're not hurt," "That didn't bother you" school?

Beyond Eighteen Months

When children become verbal, they make a transition from a kind of raw expression of signals to a more refined use of words to identify their feelings and to channel their expressions of enjoyment and distress. Parents are often startled by the bold and outspoken way their children let them know what is going on in their heads. "I hate you," "No," "Go away," can seem harsh and even hurtful. But these verbal barbs are used just as the signals for distress were—adults simply take the meaning of these words to heart much more than the meaning of preverbal signals. But in fact the wailing of a preverbal child and the statement "I hate you," may be much the same in meaning and intent: "I am angry. Something is wrong here." And a parent's tasks in managing the verbal expressions of signals are the same as earlier: Don't inhibit expression; maximize expressions of fun; and act to remove the triggers of signals for help. Don't let your emotional reactions to the word themselves cloud your judgment when it comes to responding appropriately to your newly verbal child. For more on the transition to speech, see Chapter 19.

All this may seem like a lot to take in, but as you read through the following chapters you will find yourself becoming more and more adept at observing and translating your child's signals. For example, the first time your doctor puts an X ray on the light box for you to view, it may appear to be an incomprehensible blur of black, white, and gray shapes. But then, as the doctor begins to point out various structures—"Here is an outline of your kidney, these are the vessels leading into your heart"—you can make out the inner structure of your body. And so it is with signals. I hope that the photos appearing throughout this book plus the discussions of parenting and signals will serve as your X rays into the inner emotional life of your child.

Cultivating Compatibility:

How Understanding the Signals Helps You and Your Child Get Along

Affect development and the development of cognitive skills for regulating affects are intimately related to the infant and young child's relationships with parents. Through her attunement to the behavioral emotional expressions of her infant, the primary caregiver . . . is guided to respond with appropriate caregiving and facial and other emotional expressions that, in turn, help organize and regulate the emotional life of the infant.

—Taylor, Bagby, and Parker,
Disorders of Affect Regulation

When Jennifer was about eighteen months old, not quite talking, but rather independent and aware of what was going on around her, I realized, "Hey, she's a whole lot more like her dad than like me." I mean she has his kind of sly sense of humor and tends to be observant, not so much of a participant in what's going on. It made a whole lot of things about my relationship with Jennifer suddenly click. I think I had been assuming all along that because she was a girl she was going to be like me—gregarious and a people person. I mean, I really need to be around people, to socialize a lot, to interact. And so I would thrust her into all kinds of play dates and moms' groups, and organized activities from a really young age. I couldn't stand the isolation that comes with having a new baby. But she was never all that happy in those situations. She would fuss and protest and sometimes just fall asleep. She wasn't one of those babies who was out there mixing it up with the other children. It used to drive me nuts. But when I realized she was like Richard, well, it made it easier to accept. I love him, and I enjoy spending time with him, even if we are opposites in a lot of ways. And I know how to make our two very different styles work together. I just needed to think about Jennifer the same way. It's easier to be compatible with an adult who is different from you than with a child. . . . But even so, I think there is a lot less tension between Jenny and me now. I don't get so anxious when she fusses and I am more willing

*to let her stay out of the middle of things. I hope I'm han-
dling it right. It's so hard to figure these things out as you
go along.*

—Mary Beth, thirty-three

ESTABLISHING COMPATIBILITY IS AN IMPORTANT GOAL IN YOUR
earliest relationship with your child. It allows your child to feel
that she has your approval and love and it sets the stage for the
child's happy evolution into a self-confident individual. To me,
compatibility is a comfortable, mutual affection and understanding that might be said to have three overlapping components:
(1) the establishment of healthy attachment between parent and
child; (2) a parent's acceptance of both a child's longing for
dependency and striving for autonomy; and (3), a good fit
between the parent and child.

What one hopes for is that both parent and child are able to
form a mutually beneficial dependence on one another, and the
child is able to feel secure enough to let his explorations of the
world at large blossom. This allows a child to grow into an ever
more autonomous individual, brave enough to find a happy place
in the world because he knows he can find safe harbor in his parents' care. Healthy attachment is formed when a child's needs are
attended to through appropriate responses to his nine signals. In
other words, in my view, *the nine signals—or affects or feelings—
underlie all attachment concerns and theories.*

Problems with attachment can come about in several ways. A
loving, well-meaning parent who believes in harsh discipline or
learning by hard knocks can raise a child who is insecure and

frightened. The child can grow up feeling that the parent does not offer a safe refuge, and may be reluctant to trust the parent. Or attachment can be damaged when a parent is chronically unable to understand and respond to a child's signals of interest and distress. Again, the child will be reluctant to trust the parent. On a more subtle level, a moderately depressed parent may also have a hard time establishing an alliance with her child, because the depression makes it difficult for her to pay attention to the child's needs. Whatever the cause, the results of such mismatches between parent and child may be played out over the child's lifetime in the way the child forms relationships or makes choices about work.

Another potential obstacle to attachment is related to problems with what researchers call goodness of fit. Goodness of fit refers to the degree to which parent and child are attuned to each other's basic temperament. Researchers have found that even emotionally healthy parents and children can run into difficulty if they have dramatically different styles, personalities, or temperaments. There is no assurance that your child will have the personality or character that you might pick in a close friend. For example, if a very active curious little boy or girl is born to somewhat passive parents, the parents may see the child's active behavior as overly aggressive or hyper. The parents may resent the child's active manner and label the child as difficult or troublesome. The child in turn may feel very unsupported and unable to get the gleam of approval he craves from his parents. This can put the child's developing sense of self-esteem at real risk.

Even when there are no clashes—obvious or subtle—compatibility problems can affect your family. Fortunately, this sort of problem can be overcome if you learn to respond appropriately to your child's signals and appreciate your child's unique attributes and strengths, even if they are not your own.

How Compatibility—and Incompatibility—Emerges

Interaction between parent and infant is a constant process of subtle negotiation. What the parent likes, approves of, and can tolerate is communicated to the child, either explicitly or implicitly, while the child's needs and desires are also front and center for the parents' consideration.

This ongoing negotiation is normal and important. It teaches a child patterns of communication and exchange that will form the foundation of his habits of interacting with society and other individuals. This education in communication styles starts immediately at birth and it creates a unique relationship between each parent and child. In short: Your child arrives with a set of traits that you react to; you present yourself (from a child's point of view) with a set of traits that your child reacts to; the two of you forge a relationship with each other. This dynamic process of getting to know one another, of shaping each other's experiences and attitudes, is mixed with lots of love, seasoned with good intentions and, often, a dose of confusion. That's the recipe for a family stew, and a wonderful

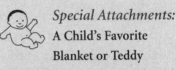

Special Attachments: **A Child's Favorite Blanket or Teddy**

Many times, as kids struggle with their feelings of attachment and swing between feelings of dependency and independence, they form strong attachments to a blanket or teddy bear. These so-called transitional objects serve many complex psychological needs: They provide a sense of love and security, can soothe upset, and may be used as a sounding board for anger and tension. Parents should allow their children to enjoy their blanket or stuffed animal for as long as they want; kids give them up when they are ready and there is little benefit in rushing the process.

dish it is. But we are often unaware of how issues around compatibility affect us.

I once knew a young mother who was having a hard time coping with her energetic son, particularly as he got somewhat older and more independent. From time to time she would bring him by to play with our son and I was a little disquieted to see that she was often impatient with his high spirits. One afternoon I asked her how she and her son were getting along.

"We get along great," Cheryl said, somewhat irritatedly. "He is everything to me. We have so much fun." But I had noticed that as he grew and became more rambunctious, Cheryl was less and less patient with him. "He can be a pretty big handful, can't he?" I suggested. "Well, yes," she confessed. "And I don't understand why he has to touch everything he sees. He can lay a room to waste in five minutes. If I take him to a playgroup, he is so aggressive. He has to be the center of everything. He overwhelms some of the kids, and I can see that the moms worry. He's just so big and strong and sociable. I hope he tones it down before he gets into grade school!"

Cheryl and her son, two very different sorts of people, are in a process of negotiation. Hopefully, they can begin to appreciate one another and to enjoy the unique qualities that they each have. It is a process that many parents go through as their child's distinct personality emerges. This becomes particularly evident when a child starts to be more independent, mobile, interacting with the world on his own terms.

"We take Holly everywhere with us, to the movies, to friends' houses, to restaurants. I've even taken her to the office with me on slow days. I believe children should be adventurous and flexible. It doesn't help them any if you keep their world too small. They need to be comfortable with people and different experiences," says Jane, twenty-eight, mother of fourteen-month-old

Holly. However, she admits, this approach is not always successful. "Sometimes she is so clingy and cries at strangers," Jane says,
slightly bewildered by her daughter's reactions. "I was talking
and walking and toilet trained by this age. I don't know why she
isn't yet."

Holly is a sensitive child, easily upset by noises, busy situations, and a lot of input. Her temperament is such that she is hap-
piest one on one, in a quiet environment, having a book read to
her or playing with one other child. She can sit for a long time in
her crib in the morning playing with toys and having conversations by herself. Jane and her daughter clearly have two different
takes on what is fun and how much stimulation they like.

Both Jane and Cheryl face challenges: It's sometimes difficult
for parents to nurture and encourage personality traits in children who are so different from themselves. But trying to squelch
or reshape a child's natural way of encountering the world can set
up a conflict of wills and make the child feel unworthy, ashamed,
and/or confused about his or her essential self.

In some instances, the difficulties with compatibility are
caused by a parent's own emotional problems. Louise is slightly
depressed and uncomfortable with being the center of attention.
She has a two-year-old child, Katie, however, who is a natural
born star—a pretty, outgoing girl who thrives on interaction with
the world. This thrusts Louise into the spotlight far more than
she is comfortable with. "She is just uncontrollable," Louise says.
"Everyone is always coming up to talk to her, and she is always
running around to see everything. Sometimes it drives me crazy."
Even at this early stage of their relationship, you can see that they
are destined to butt heads. Unless Louise learns to appreciate
Katie's best qualities and accept her for who she is, Katie is going
to have to fight for her own territory, and that can lead to a lot of
unhappiness on both sides. In this instance, Louise's depression is

an additional difficulty, for Louise is not the master of her own self and doesn't have good self-esteem. Often children of parents who are depressed grow up feeling that they must work extra hard to make their parent happy and put the parent's needs before their own. In such a situation, a child may learn quickly that the only way he can get his own psychological needs met is to cheer up his melancholy parent or become compliant in more complicated ways. He may take on the role of family clown. This exacts a toll on the child if it goes on for too long a time. The child learns to organize his personality around the needs of the parent. His own creativity and assets may be shortchanged in the process.

If you think you may suffer from depression, or any other emotional problem, it is essential for yourself and your child that you seek help; depression and other emotional problems do not have to be accepted. They can be treated and you can make your life and your child's life a lot happier.

How to Cultivate Compatibility

If Cheryl or Jane or Louise reminds you of yourself, there are positive steps you can take to improve compatibility with your child. Just as the love between you and your partner deepens over time as you learn to understand and appreciate one another more, your relationship with your child is enriched when you accept some traits, and admire or delight in others.

The first important step in dealing with the compatibility dilemma is to become aware of the problem. In other words, the trick is to realize that different styles might exist, and that these differences do not mean that the two of you cannot cherish, admire, and enjoy each other. Rather you will grow to see that though you have different styles, different energy levels, you can adjust to these differences. This will help you avoid the harmful cycle of feeling that either one of you are wrong or bad. The second step is to use the information about the nine signals, and things flow pretty readily from there.

The Benefits of Cultivating Compatibility

No matter if you and your child must work to forge an understanding of one another or to get in sync, you both will reap great rewards from deepening your understanding and appreciation of each other's individual characteristics. The improved compatibility that results will keep you and your child from getting on each other's nerves. It allows you each to express your feelings and then move through them to resolution and understanding. It helps limit distress and keeps the joy of parenthood alive. And as a result, both you and your child are able to regulate tension: You may be better able to regulate your emotional responses to your child and your child will learn through your positive example to modulate his feelings as well. Together you will build a mutual pleasure in sharing intimate feelings and exploring the world around you.

Encouraging Playfulness

Donald Winnicott, a British pediatrician turned psychoanalyst, once commented: "Psychotherapy is done in the overlap of the two play areas, that of the patient and that of the
therapist." I would paraphrase this and suggest: "Parenting
is done in the overlap of two play areas, that of the parent
and that of the child."

—Paul C. Holinger

When Susan was about ten months old she began to be
afraid of strangers and was often upset when we went out to
the grocery store or the mall. This wonderful, happy baby
was suddenly a handful and I didn't know what to do or how
to handle it. It really was frustrating and I got impatient
with her. I mean there wasn't anything actually frightening
out there! But I didn't know how to convince her to calm

down. For a while I stopped taking her out with me. We stayed home a lot and it was driving me stir-crazy. Then one day my friend came over and convinced me to take Susan with us to go shopping. Of course the minute we hit the department store floor, she started fussing and crying. I was ready to turn around and go home. But then a wonderful thing happened. My friend wheeled her stroller over to a little waterfall that was by the front door and sat down next to her and began talking all about the water. She put her hand in it and splashed it, then she got up and went to the other side and looked at Susan through the falling water. They spent about five minutes doing that. Then my friend moved the stroller about ten feet further into the store and stopped by a rack of clothes. She took Susan's hand and let her touch the fabrics. They talked about colors. They rattled the hangers. Then they went a little further and looked into a case with some flashy jewelry in it. That was an occasion for another discussion. She motioned me over to them and got me involved in the scene. After a while Susan started looking around at what else there was to explore. She gestured toward another rack of clothes. I wheeled her over there. It might have taken fifteen minutes, but it was terrific. She was really having fun examining everything with us. It broke the ice and we were able to spend about an hour shopping without Susan getting too fussy. When I talked to my friend about it afterwards I realized that I had been feeling so embarrassed by Susan's tantrums when I would take her to the store that I hadn't been able to step back and figure out how to solve the problem. A little fun and games was all that was required but I was too upset to think of it. I just thought it was all my fault and I wanted to get out of the situation as fast as possible.

—Cary, twenty-eight,
a first-time mother

PLAYFULNESS, A SENSE OF FUN IN MANY SITUATIONS, COMES FROM the interplay of your child's signals for interest, enjoyment, and surprise. When it is present, it allows for emotional flexibility and delight in encountering the world. I think that it may be one of the most important elements in raising an emotionally healthy child. I recommend a wonderful book, *Playful Parenting,* by Lawrence Cohen, which is organized around the concept of play in parenting. This idea of playfulness is quite consistent with the stimulus-seeking nature of the brain.

Parents can use playfulness to manage the signals for help, such as distress and anger, to dispel daily tension, and to handle frustration. In fact, the ability to be playful has an impact in all areas of life. For example, it affects career choice: People who have a sense of what they are interested in and what they enjoy— who have the ability to be playful—are those who can ultimately do what they genuinely love to do, who can make their everyday lives meaningful.

Some parents and caregivers have more playful personalities

than others. However, even parents who tend to be more serious can readily learn to lighten up their interaction with their baby and get their infant laughing and smiling.

If you pay attention to what your child enjoys you will be able to develop a playful relationship. Most younger children respond positively to stimulation of their senses of touch, sight, and hearing. Think of how a baby responds to peek-a-boo, goofy faces, or changes in rhythm and tone of voice. Basically, children find interest and enjoyment in any activity that creates a nonstartling shift in the intensity of their sensory perception—from soft to a bit louder, or slow to somewhat faster. For example, a baby will usually giggle and laugh if you slowly and soothingly sing the beginning of "Rock-a-bye Baby" and then finish up the phrase by rapidly crooning "in the treetop," perhaps shaking your head or moving quickly toward the baby as the words speed up.

Older children delight in slightly bolder actions such as being raised up in the air and then held tightly to your chest, or riding your knee like a galloping horse and then having the pace change and slow to a rolling lope. Toddlers love playing catch, riding on swings, or motoring around on tricycles.

How Playfulness
Helps Ease Upsets

In day-to-day situations, the spirit of playfulness can be used to distract an infant or older child from distress. For example, babies sometimes get fussy or distressed when their diapers are changed or they are dressed. This can be difficult for parents who must perform those activities. They can't remove the trigger of their baby's distress. They have to go through with it. But if Mom or Dad can introduce playfulness into the situation, rather than get frustrated and impatient, then baby can shift his mood too.

For example, it can work wonders if pulling the T-shirt over baby's head becomes a time to play peek-a-boo or if you offer baby the cardboard roller from a roll of paper towels to play with while you change the diaper. You might also put on a record and sing along, or talk about what's in the room, or tell a story. Anything that provides interest and enjoyment will lighten the atmosphere.

Bedtime is another situation that goes a lot smoother if you use playfulness to ease signals of distress. "When Jay was a year and a half old he hated to go to bed," remembers his mom, Sandi. "He was so afraid he was missing out on something going on in the other room. So we developed a game with his stuffed animals. I'd tuck them under the covers in his bed, and then I'd say, 'Oh Jaaay. I think I hear something,' and bark like a dog. Jay would look kind of perplexed. Then I'd ask him who that could be. 'Do I hear Sammy and Jimmy?' I'd say. Well, that would do it. He'd squeal and I'd bark some more. He'd try to bark too. We'd go in search of his animals, and when he found them, after we looked all around the house, he would dive into the crib to snuggle with them. I think because we went throughout the house, and made it all so interesting, he was able to forget about what he might be missing out there somewhere and could focus on his bed and his animals."

Babies are also easily distressed when they are bored. Their whole being is a sensory input machine—they love to receive stimulation from their surroundings and other people. That's why they are so intrigued by an endless parade of everyday objects—a magazine, pots and pans, your hair, their toes, something shiny. But when they are in a situation where they are understimulated, they quickly become restless and then agitated. Being stuck in a stroller wheeling through narrow store aisles, where they can't touch anything or see much, can produce wails of unhappiness. Take time to offer them some interesting and enjoyable stimulation—a toy, a conversation, a chance to touch what they see, a funny song—and they will calm down.

Kids Learn Playfulness by Your Example. When you are frustrated, if you make an effort to react with interest and enjoyment, your child will learn a valuable lesson in using playfulness to handle frustration—and you'll end up feeling better too. For example, finding what is amusing or entertaining in a traffic jam will give your child a good lesson in how and when to be playful. As frustration mounts you may say, "This is getting to be a real pain. But if we're stuck here, let's sing a song." Your response offers a clear demonstration of how to cope with agitation.

This ability to use playfulness to transform distress is a powerful way to help your child develop tension regulation. For example, when you and your child are stuck in the waiting room at the doctor's and frustration is growing, take the opportunity to turn the passing minutes into playtime, reading magazines, playing hide and seek, walking around the room, and looking at the pictures on the wall. By using these examples, or by using paper and pencil to draw pictures, you will help your child find new ways to cope with stress and boredom.

Kids Learn Playfulness by Your Responses to Their Signals. Children also develop playfulness when parents react appropriately to their child's signals and then follow up with a moment of fun. For example, if there is a loud noise—a car alarm goes off right in your child's ear as you are pushing the stroller down the street—your baby may express surprise and then fear. How he reacts depends on his innate sensitivity and a combination of circumstances: (1) whether or not you acted promptly to offer protection and comfort from the noise, (2) whether or not you took the time to put words to the situation, and help the child learn to express anxiety using language, and (3) if you found a way to transform the alarm into something amusing. You might imitate the sound of the horn, or make funny faces at the upsetting noise, or wave good-bye to the offending car as you walk quickly away. These kinds of extra gestures help the child overcome her initial surprise, gain some sense of mastery over the threatening situation, and find ways to transform the alarm into something amusing.

So next time a big dog scares your baby, take him quickly out of harm's way, offer reassurance and sympathy, and then distract him with something that is fun and lighthearted—a song about the dog, a quick jog down the street in your arms, a chance to look at himself in a window.

Surprise is not the only signal, however, that offers a chance to teach playfulness. Each and every signal presents parents with a chance to encourage playfulness, and to improve tension regulation. Kids who don't feel that parents respond attentively to their signals often increase the emotional ante, intensifying their signals, becoming more agitated and less playful. Even the signals for interest and enjoyment, when not attended to appropriately, can spin out of control.

When Playfulness Seems Like Willfulness

Sometimes play strikes parents as misbehaving or defying authority, instead of interest and enjoyment. For instance, if your eighteen-month-old child is pulling canned goods off the pantry shelf, it probably doesn't look like good clean play to you. But to your child this is great fun. He is exploring something interesting. He is enjoying the crash of the cans as they roll to the floor. His senses are engaged. So, when you interrupt the activity, no wonder he howls. Many times, he may go back to pulling the cans off the shelf, apparently defying you. But step back a moment and observe your child. Chances are you'll see that he is not just throwing cans around willy-nilly. He is investigating a new treasure trove. Mastering the art of picking up and throwing things. Learning about up and down and crash and boom. And all the while he is also looking for your reaction. He's asking you, "Do I really have to stop playing?" "How serious are you?" "Are you going to yell or get mad?" This is the beginning of a second kind of play—your baby is playing with you and he is trying to get you to play with him, to participate in the delightful and interesting activity. So stop and ask yourself, "Does my son really need to stop?" And if he does, "What else can I find for him to do that is fun and will provide the same stimulation?"

"I Want to Be Like You, Mom and Dad!":

How and Why Children Identify with Their Parents

My son used to love to "shave" with me. I would help him lather up his cheeks and give him an empty razor so he could pretend. But, on a busy morning, it was easy to forget how important his drive to imitate my behavior really was, and how much of a compliment it was, too. As the minutes ticked by, I would try to remember this, however, and to encourage and support his play-acting. I would guess most parents have had the same experience. To remain patient, I would remind myself about just how much of a role model parents are to their children and what a big help it can be in cementing the relationship and providing guidance. Keeping this in mind helped prevent me from misunderstanding my son's

imitative behavior and from injuring his good-hearted
impulse to be like me and be liked by me.

—Paul C. Holinger

YOUR CHILD'S TENDENCY TO WANT TO BE LIKE MOM AND DAD IS one of the most powerful influences on his emerging character. In fact, your baby's tremendous conscious and unconscious urge to emulate you is one of the strongest, and perhaps most often overlooked, motivators of behavior. This inherent impulse to identify with you can be a tremendous help in raising an emotionally healthy child.

What's behind an infant's tendency to imitate and identify with parents? The answer takes us into a much studied and somewhat complicated aspect of infant development. Charles Darwin (1809–1882) was much intrigued by the strength of imitative tendencies in both animals and man, and Sigmund Freud (1856–1939) studied these processes in depth from a psychological perspective. More recently, researchers have explored the tendencies of infants to identify with and emulate the important people in their lives. These studies suggest that at a very early age much of a child's well-being and sense of belonging comes from the feeling that "I am like my parent" and "My parent is like me." Parents too have these feelings of "likeness" with their children. And it is this exchange of identification that gives a child a feeling of kinship and leads to a child's idealization of the parents. These are complex dynamics. Even sorting out words such as "identification," "imitation," "mimic," and the phrase "to be like" is more than we need to take on—each has a distinct meaning in the world of child psychology. However, for this discussion, I will use the words interchangeably and with their everyday conversational meanings.

How Your Child Sees You

Babies always seem most interested in what you have or what you are doing. They want to play with the shaving cream or use the toothbrush. As a parent, you can use this tendency to teach the baby a variety of things. For example, what better way to teach your child to wash his hands or brush his teeth than to do it first yourself. "See Mommy brushing her teeth like this. Uppers. Lowers. Oh, you want to play with this? Okay, here we go." Or, if you have to struggle to get your child to allow you to clip her nails, you can try showing her how you clip yours, first. "See? Clip this one, and this one. Now, do you want to try? Okay, here we go. Let me hold it with you and we'll do it together. Very good." Imitation can also help make haircuts an easier process. They are often a real trial, because of the newness of the situation, the rapid movements toward the child's head and eyes, and the use of scissors, which have been the subject of loud warnings such as "Sharp! Be careful." The solution? Try sitting in the barber's chair and get a little trim first. Pretty soon your child will be clamoring to get in the chair or on your lap and have a haircut too.

Children learn more than simple tasks through their impulse to imitate you. They use imitation and identification to pick up a lot more complex and subtle information. Much of your child's character is formed by the tendency to imitate your worldview, emotional expressions, and attitudes. She inevitably picks up your habits regarding tension regulation, playfulness, learning, interpersonal relationships, and expression of affection. That's why being affectionate and honest in your dealings with your child and other people will help tremendously in raising an affectionate and honest child. Telling your child, "Don't lie," or "Be nice!" is much less effective than telling the truth and being kind yourself. You'll discover very quickly the wisdom of "actions speak louder than words" and "practice what you preach." As a dad once told me, "I sure learned in a hurry to watch my bad habits once Charlie was around."

Other ways to use identification to help your child develop include:

Demonstrating Tension Regulation: If you are able to modulate your emotions, so that you don't fly off the handle when you are frustrated, your child has a better chance of learning to do the same. If, on the other hand, you are given to outbursts of anger or yelling, chronic impatience and irritation, shows of disgust, then your child will think that is the right way to handle stressful situations. If you don't have good tension regulation yourself, then chances are there will be at least two people—you and your child—in the house who don't know how to defuse a tense situation or soothe their frazzled nerves. That can make for a lot of bickering, ill will, and mutual frustration. All of this really gets back to understanding and dealing reasonably with the foundation of emotional life—the nine built-in signals.

Playful Is as Playful Does: As we discussed in Chapter 6 on playfulness, being able to find interest and enjoyment in a wide variety of circumstances—even those that are stressful, such as a traffic jam—teaches your child useful ways of regulating tension, and makes the world a more interesting and rewarding place.

Instilling the Love of Learning: If you have a curious mind and enjoy reading, taking classes, figuring out how to build things, or discussing ideas and world events, you will provide a role model for your child that will bring a lifetime of pleasure and reward. When the two of you watch TV, keep a dictionary, encyclopedia, or computer handy so you can look up words, or historical figures, or find more information on a subject. Make a game out of it. When you travel, make an effort to show your child maps of where you are going, explain geography, and encourage questions about where you are and what you see.

Showing Your Child How to Express Affection and How to Be a Good Friend: The ability to have satisfying intimate relationships is learned, in part, through the way parents relate to their children, to one another, and to their friends. If you are able to show affection and to be both sympathetic and empathic, then your child will not only receive the benefits of your warm nature, he will also learn how to form intimate relationships.

Translating Actions and Feelings into Words: As mentioned earlier, labeling feelings and substituting words for actions greatly enhances the emotional and cognitive development of a young child. Talking to your child about what you are thinking and feeling and labeling your child's signals and emotions for him from a very early age will help him learn how to manage emotions and use the metaphor of language to express intense emotions as early as possible. You can help your child develop this skill by making sure you actively use words to communicate your feelings and as a substitute for actions. For example, when you are angry, if you express your feelings using reasonable words that convey your thoughts instead of throwing things or ranting, then your child will learn to do the same.

Including Your Child in Decision-Making Situations: From an early age you can help your child gain confidence in his ability to identify and express what he thinks, wants, and believes by asking him to participate in everyday decision making. Even toddlers can be allowed input in a family decision: Go to the grocery store or to a restaurant for dinner? Make a peanut butter or tuna fish sandwich for lunch? Wear your pink socks or your blue ones? It may make life less efficient in the short run, but in the long run you will teach your child about the decision-making process, weighing pros and cons, and that you value his opinion and trust his judgment.

Using Imitation and Identification to Help Develop Manners: Manners are important for children. Not only do they make it easier for children to find acceptance and make friends, but manners also teach boundaries and remind them that other people's feelings and needs are important. Even before your child learns to talk, they can pick up the nuances that are communicated when people treat one another with respect and care. You have the chance to set a tone that she will bring into her world of words and language as she matures. But how often have you heard parents admonish a child, "say please," "say thank you," "say you're sorry," "hold the door for that person," but without saying or doing those things themselves? If you want your child to learn manners, things will go much easier if you demonstrate the behavior instead of talking just about it. If you treat your child politely and say, "Sweetheart, would you please pick that apple up off the floor?" or "Thank you for closing the door," the child will be much more likely to act politely as she gets older.

Children also learn to apologize and acknowledge a mistake without being defensive by watching how you handle your mistakes. If you say, "Oh, I am so sorry I pinched your finger in the high chair," or, "Honey, I am very sorry I dropped your toy car and chipped the headlight. Should I try to fix it?" then they will grow up with a graceful style of handling their own missteps.

Using humor and appealing to your child's self-interest are also good ways to teach manners. If you want your preverbal child to learn to say please, you can turn it into a fun sounding game: "Honey, will you pleeeeeze give me that book?" makes the word funny and entertaining. It catches the child's attention and teaches a lesson using playfulness.

Beyond Modeling Behavior: Teaching Decision Making

Imitation can also be used to help your child develop good decision-making skills so he can sort out feelings and select the most appropriate option for responding. Manners, tension regulation, and playfulness are all important examples of the ability to make a good decision about how to handle complex interactions and internal emotions.

Here again, kids pick up a lot of their habits about decision making from watching you. If you impose rules on a child, "because I say so," then the child will learn that arbitrary-seeming responses are the way to behave. One day, when you ask why on earth your child has done this or that, the toddler will look at you and say, "Because I want to," and feel that is a reasonable explanation. Being authoritarian toward your child may be mirrored back at you in the form of stubbornness and inflexibility. That's why over and over I have stressed the importance of labeling and explaining your directives to your child. When you tell a child to do or not do something, set out your reasons for it in a calm, loving voice. Don't hesitate to say, even to the youngest infant, "I don't want you to do that because I love you and I don't want you to get hurt." Or, "You can't have that because that is something

that is valuable to Daddy and he would be sad if it was ruined."
Explain why. Talk about what you believe and feel. Take the time
to communicate instead of trying to end a situation quickly and
moving on. If you operate with the unstated message that sharing
thoughts and discussing reasons for decisions is a waste of time,
your child will pick up on that. But if you explain why you do
things or think thoughts, then the child will understand that you
think things through and will learn to do the same himself.

Common Misunderstandings

Parents can easily misunderstand a child's desire to imitate their
behavior. It is an injustice that can stick with a child her whole
life. Many times, when I ask parents to recall an early conflict
with their parents, they mention being misunderstood when
they were simply trying to act like their mom or dad. Yet, ironically, with their own kids, they fall into the common trap of seeing an action as "misbehavior," when it is often no more than
innocent imitation. One child I knew was always playing with
the buttons on her parents' alarm clock before she went to bed.
Her father was getting angry about it, until her mother realized
that the child was simply doing what she'd seen her father do
when he was getting ready for bed. Their clever solution was to
put an old alarm clock in the child's bedroom so she could "set"
it for herself.

A father of a two-year-old boy was convinced that his son was
learning how to steal money when he found him going through
his work pants and taking out his wallet, keys, and coins. The
father was going to punish the boy rather severely, until a friend
suggested that the little boy was just doing what his father did.
"He's trying to be a grown-up man, just like you. He's putting his
wallet, change, and keys in his pockets and getting ready for

work." The dad then bought his son a pair of overalls with a front pocket and gave him a little wallet with a couple of dollar bills, some coins, and old keys. He made a point of putting his pants on the same time as his son did and they both put their keys and money into their pockets. Sharing the activity delighted his son, and his so-called stealing was correctly understood to be playful identification with dad. The father validated his child's desire to imitate him, but he also took advantage of the situation to impart an important lesson in manners and behavior. He explained to his son that it is not a good idea to take money or anything else that belongs to another person. "You need to ask first, and explain why you want it," he told him.

Potential Trouble Spots: When Children Imitate Parents' Misbehavior

Since an infant child cannot discriminate between your attributes that are worth copying and those that might be better left alone, it is useful to be aware of the negative traits that you might be teaching your child—some of which you may have picked up from your own parents. You may want to take an inventory of how you express the nine signals—interest, enjoyment, surprise, distress, anger, fear, shame, disgust, and dissmell. And take some time to reflect on your own behavior and to think about any personal habits or qualities that you may want to change, improve, or mitigate. Your power to mold your child's attitudes, emotions, and behavior is so great that it is wise to try to make sure you are transmitting messages that you want your child to receive.

First-time moms often experience a kind of déjà vu. When I asked a friend if she was aware of how much children identify with and imitate their parents she exclaimed: "It's so true—now that I have Clöe, I realize how much I am like my parents, how much I absorbed from them. These are things that I was only vaguely aware of—and some of them are not so good. But now I see how I get agitated over small things like my mom and how I tune out like my dad. I hope I can stop being so much like my parents so Clöe won't learn the same bad habits from me."

Luckily people can change and grow. I am reminded of a Hall of Fame hockey player who used to rack up two hundred penalty minutes a year. He was a notorious brawler. Eventually he married and had a daughter. When she was around three years old, she started watching him play on TV. He'd never felt the slightest compunction before about his on-ice behavior, but one day she asked, "Daddy, why do you fight so much?" Suddenly he was horrified at the thought that she was seeing him hit other players and get into fistfights. So he changed how he played. From that day on he was more contained on the ice; in fact he won several league awards for sportsmanship and leadership and his reputation as a player didn't suffer at all. He credits his daughter with teaching him two valuable lessons, one about being a parent and the other about playing hockey.

While you may try to modify your less desirable traits, you need to be aware that what you think are your most muted, hidden emotions and unconscious actions may nonetheless be coming through loud and clear. Infants can pick up aspects of your emotions, worldview, and physical actions that you may not even be aware of consciously. For example, some parents who profess open-mindedness, but are actually intolerant or prejudiced, often end up with equally intolerant kids. The children may hear lip service given to civil rights, for example, but the message that some people are inferior comes across in gestures, expressions, and word choices. Children adopt the same prejudiced point of view, even if they are too young to actually know what it means.

We had a neighbor when we were first married who was cordial and well mannered but filled with all kinds of biases about people. In casual conversation he'd say things like, "you know how the [fill in an ethnic or racial group] are," or "that was as dirty as a [fill in an ethnic or racial group]." It was a bit stunning to hear his three-year-old son mouth the same upsetting stereotypes.

There have been some interesting and successful attempts to counter prejudice in young children. A wonderful book by Vivian Gussin Paley, *You Can't Say You Can't Play*, tells the story of what happened in an elementary school when a teacher decided to make it a rule that no child could tell another that he or she was excluded from a group activity. All the kids—including those that were sometimes singled out as different because of race, appearance, or behavior—were to be included. At first, many children resented the rules, and they wrestled with issues of inclusion, exclusion, rejection, and fairness. But over time they discovered that they could enjoy everyone's company and learn from those kids who were different. The class developed much more harmony and fewer cliques.

Imitation: Another Reason Not to Abuse

A child who is hit or otherwise abused is likely to have negative feelings of anger, distress, and fear stirred up, and these interfere with healthy, normal development. In addition, an abused child may also adopt the very behavior that is hurting him and become abusive himself. He may see hitting as a normal and acceptable way to solve problems and get what he wants. And not only will the child become mean to others, he may become mean to himself. Abused children often turn the impulse to hit onto themselves and adopt various self-destructive behaviors and relationships.

Your Child Wants to Be Like You,
but She Is Different!

Parents gain a great deal by recognizing how much their children want to be like them, but they also need to remember how unlike them their child is. These differences are not just matters of taste and pace and different strokes for different folks, but also of age-related mental abilities. Young children do not have the same capacities as adults to understand and remember what is safe and what is not, what can be played with and what cannot, and so on. They simply haven't developed the impulse control or cognitive abilities to understand that they are not supposed to be playing with electric wires or the contents of the refrigerator. This can cause a lot of frustration in parents who aren't aware that this exploring is a natural and normal stage of development, best managed by offering the child other equally intriguing alternatives to play with, not a scolding or worse.

As Your Child Grows Older

Your child's impulse to identify with you does not stop with childhood. You can continue to use it to help your child navigate successfully through adolescence and into adulthood. With teens, lessons in moderation and responsible behavior, respect for one's own health, and an interest in ideas and other people are often best transmitted through example instead of words—particularly if they learned through example as infants. That doesn't mean that identification will make it easy to teach your teen to act wisely or to dial down impulsiveness. Much of adolescent behavior is the result of a struggle between a teen's desire for independence, on the one hand, and closeness to parents on the other. It turns out you are more of a role model than you may know, and this can have far-reaching benefits to your child and to you as well.

A friend of mine found he was constantly getting into verbal fights with his teenage son because the boy would borrow hats, ties, jackets, and coats without asking. It was only when I suggested that perhaps his son was simply trying to get close to his dad, to be like him, that the father was able to see the nice side to having his closet plundered and to appreciate his son's well-meaning though irritating behavior. There were a lot fewer fights after that, although the father did have to struggle to get his son to learn to ask before taking the clothing. In time, they even went shopping together and started spending more time together playing sports. "I never expected to be so close to Sean at this age," he says now. "I just thought I'd be the enemy until he was about twenty-five. I can't tell you how glad I am that I took the time to understand what was behind his raids on my closet."

Teenagers borrow their parents' clothing, wear makeup like an adult, and try out adult experiences such as drinking and sex, often because they want to identify with their parents, for good or for bad. They also search for mentors and idealized heroes who help them define their own personalities more clearly during the upheavals of adolescence. This is all part of a complicated pattern of identification and imitation. So take a deep breath, and remember that when you mess up, it's just one more opportunity to help your child learn decision making, how to apologize, and humility. You'll discover that there are a lot fewer parenting mistakes if you just make them part of the learning experience.

Building Your Child's Self-Esteem

Self-esteem is something that's hard to notice in an infant. But now that my son is fifteen, I can see the contrast between him and some of his friends, and I think it is directly related to this whole issue of how much belief he has in himself. I see it in the kids' body language. He stands tall, looks you in the eye when he speaks, is comfortable with adults. But he has a friend, a nice bright kid, who is like a mole. He ducks his head, his appearance is kind of messy, and I can't get him to talk to my wife or me. You hurt for him, it seems like it's so hard for him to make his way through a day. And you just know he's beaten down somehow. I've talked to my son about this and he tells me that his friend's parents don't really have time or patience or interest in their son. From the outside it is confusing. I know the parents and they are very nice folks, with a lot on the ball. It has to be that there are a

whole lot of very subtle, long-term behaviors and attitudes
going on between parents and son that have undermined
that kid. I don't think the parents have a clue about what
they've done to make their son so insecure, certainly nothing
intentional. Parenting is really tough, even for the most well
meaning.

—Dave, forty-three

A NEW BABY IS BORN WITH CERTAIN NEUROLOGICAL CAPACITIES and resulting temperament and talents, but she doesn't have a solid sense of who she is or what her place is in the world. The slow building of a sense of self, and of a sense of one's position in the world, comes about through the passage of time and the accumulation of experience. When a baby finds that her signals are validated and responded to appropriately—that troubles are soothed and pleasure enhanced—she begins to sense that her feelings, expressions of her very being, are of value and important. A baby learns that she counts for something. This is the foundation of the development of self-esteem—a combination of who you are, how you feel about yourself, and what you think about your future potential.

Clearly, self-esteem is an essential building block of emotional health and a happy, successful life. And, as with so many of the important components of a child's development, self-esteem also takes root or withers depending on how you handle your child's nine signals, maximizing the signals of fun—interest and enjoyment—and validating and attending to the signals for help—distress, anger, fear, shame, disgust, and dissmell.

As parents you are the most important people in your baby's world. You provide your child with his first definitions of himself. You tell him through your every word, gesture, and action just how important he is and how he is perceived by the outside world. If he cries when he is hungry and you feed him, you tell him his most basic needs can be fulfilled. If he laughs, and you delight in his enjoyment, you tell him he is right to find pleasure in life's little moments of discovery. The accumulation of these positive messages helps him have confidence in feelings and his perceptions of the world at large. They lay the foundation for self-esteem.

Over the coming months and years, as your child matures and becomes an adult, his self-esteem will become a more complex web of interlocking emotions and thoughts about himself and about how he sees and is seen by others. Although you might want to shield him from any bruises to his self-esteem, life seems to dent everyone's self-confidence at one time or another. Bring home bad grades, break up with a girlfriend, or—later on—get fired from a job, and your son may say, "I don't feel so good about myself."

Conversely, short-term bursts of self-esteem can come from good fortune and achievement. Acceptance or success at school, for example, can boost self-esteem—or even overinflate it. In fact, it's common for growing children and as well as adults to fluctuate between episodes of high and low self-esteem over the course of months or years. However, a solid foundation of self-esteem—built by appropriate responses to a child's signals and nurtured throughout childhood—will help most people maintain a basically optimistic view of their lives and their future over the course of life's ups and downs.

Your goal now, with your baby, is to help him develop a sense of himself that is reasonably solid and stable. As he grows, that will allow him to perceive his talents and abilities accurately, respond to life with flexibility, and look at his goals and capacities realistically. It may help him become a person who is open to new ideas and allow him to acknowledge when he is wrong. This kind of development is important if he is able to love others in a generous, genuine, wholehearted way.

Of course, the real key is loving the very essence of your child—loving and valuing the child for himself or herself, who he or she *is*. But this is often easier said than done—especially if the parents have not been loved and valued. Yet, understanding the nine signals can be useful here too: Much of the child's essence is wrapped up in her interests and enjoyments; and understanding and attending to the negative signals can help prevent the cycles of frustration, hurt, and anger which can so contaminate the parent-child relationship and erode the child's internal world.

The Foundations of Self-Esteem

From the first days of your baby's life, you can lay the foundation for self-esteem by responding appropriately to your child's signals for help (distress, anger, etc.) and fun (interest and enjoyment). When you validate your child's signals, you help the child gain confidence in her perception of the world and his feelings; you also nurture tension regulation and help her interact capably with the external world.

Many experts believe that another important building block of self-esteem involves a child's experience of competence. Competence, as described by the pioneer psychoanalytic researcher Dr. Michael Basch, is initially achieved as a result of the brain's capacity to create order out of the disorder of all the incoming stimuli. An infant's inherent ability to develop competence lays the foundation for later, more sophisticated mastery of interaction with the world and people, which in turn may produce a sense of self-esteem. One part of this development, as a child grows, is learning that he is able to exert control over external events. Another, as he interacts with his environment, is learning how to adapt in a healthy way to the external world's social requirements and expectations.

How to Help Your Child
Build Self-Esteem

If you express admiration and take pleasure in your infant's "accomplishments," particularly about things that elicit your baby's enthusiasm, you will do a great deal to instill a sense of competence and self-confidence. But there are other useful tools for building self-esteem as well.

Focusing Appropriate Attention on the Child. Babies thrive when they feel they are of genuine interest to you and are the center of your universe. They use their nine signals to express their entire range of emotions. But their experience of the outside world and their interaction with it is limited—they feel interest, for example, but only in what is right in front of them. They feel distress, say, when they have gas, and wail with as much intensity as an adult would over a considerably more dramatic upset. Their emotions, whether positive or negative, are stimulated by their own immediate experiences. This gives each feeling a heightened immediacy and importance. That's why when a baby cries, or fusses, or coos, she expects you to react with as much enthusiasm or distress as she does about what is happening to her.

As babies get older and are able to crawl and walk, they exhibit the same endless curiosity they had about what was nearest to them, only now they focus on the most ordinary objects: pots, pans, magazines, pieces of lint. They grab, pull, and put the most troubling things in their mouths, because these are the ways they have to explore what they encounter.

They expand their reactions to things that cause them distress as well. Now in addition to gas bubbles, they may express distress about large dogs, loud noises, unusual looking people, or the inability to reach objects that catch their attention. As their interaction with the world expands, the list of events that can provoke crying and anger gets longer and more complex. What parents sometimes forget is that to babies those reactions of distress are proportional to the situation. Not being able to get ahold of a ball that rolled into a corner is terrible! And your baby wants you to pay attention to him when he announces it in no uncertain terms. He finds himself incapable of righting the situation himself—no matter what he does, he'll never be able to reach the ball. Talk about frustration! So he asks for your help in the only way he can—by making a scene. If that doesn't elicit your sympathy and attention, if you don't respond and help your baby out of his distress, he will begin to think that his problems don't really matter, how he feels doesn't count. Instead, if you take the opportunity to pay attention, validating and confirming his feelings and perceptions, you will help your child become confident. Dismiss the calls for attention often enough and problems may develop. Donald Winnicott, the pediatrician turned psychoanalyst, suggested that if a parent praises a child's interest and enjoyment only when they coincide with the parent's own, a child may forsake his own genuine feelings of interest and enjoyment and develop a false self in order to please the parent. The result is that the child's accurate sense of himself, and of self-esteem, is undermined.

Provide Reward and Praise. Along with paying attention, reward and praise from you are essential to a child's self-esteem. You must never forget how much your child wants to be like you and to be liked by you. Kids need to hear that you approve of them and think they are wonderful. They long to see that "gleam in your eye" that signals love and approval. You can't assume they know how you feel. They don't. They need to be told, over and over and over. In the long run, reward and praise tend to be better and healthier motivators than fear and shame. Of course, whenever you're dealing with behavior, it is also important to explain to the child the pros and cons, the reasons and rationales, for whatever issue is at stake.

Offer Protection. If a child perceives the world as threatening or dangerous, it is almost impossible for her to feel brave and strong, to know that she can make her way through it successfully. But when you respond to your child's negative signals of distress and anger by allowing expression of the signals and then removing the triggers, you have begun to give her the tools to deal with the world. When it comes to feeling confident, nothing helps a helpless baby like knowing that she can depend on you to shield her from danger and distress.

How Self-Esteem Is Damaged

Some parents inadvertently diminish their children's self-esteem by interfering with or belittling their signals for interest and enjoyment. This triggers the automatic, built-in response of shame, and shame erodes self-esteem. Chapter 17, on shame, explains how this happens in more detail.

In my clinical practice, I frequently work with families in which both the parents and children have a variety of troubles related to a poor sense of self and self-esteem. What I have observed is that the adults in these families often have trouble identifying their own emotions and cannot accurately perceive those of others. They don't understand how feelings and emotions work. The family ends up in a toxic situation because there is a mismatch between the child's expression of emotional needs and the parent's ability to respond appropriately. Often, then, the children fail to develop a solid sense of self—who they are, what they like and don't like, a confidence in their perceptions and feelings, and so on. When parents are not able to respond in helpful ways to their child's expressions of both positive and negative signals, the child may misunderstand his parents' signals—yes, parents have these signals too. The resulting tension that develops between parent and child can contribute to the erosion of his self-esteem. The child may become angry, defensive, intolerant, and inflexible, or withdrawn, self-destructive, envious, and fearful. Some children develop an overinflated sense of self-importance—known technically as compensatory grandiosity—as they try to make up for their lack of self-esteem. Adults, too, may compensate for an internal lack of solid self-esteem by becoming inappropriately grandiose, arrogant, and intolerant. In fact, a whole variety of the less pleasing personality traits can be directly attributed to a person's lack of belief in his own essential worth. Think bully. Think timid. Think depressed, depleted, and drained. These different qualities result, in part, from a lack of self-esteem.

The results of these kinds of parenting missteps can be heartbreaking. But the results of positive parenting are tremendous. You and your child are able to enjoy one another's company, to delight in the deepening of your friendship. You gain access to the delightfully quirky way the world looks to a child. You learn as your baby learns. You gain confidence in your parenting skills; your self-esteem increases. Over time, you become ever more able to allow your child to grow into a unique, self-confident being. And because she has a solid sense of self, she will become capable of forming fulfilling relationships and of maintaining a healthy autonomy.

Turning Off Your Parenting Autopilot . . . :

Identifying and Dealing with Your Assumptions About Being a Mom or a Dad

I wasn't very comfortable with our baby when he first came home. I was glad Harry Junior was there and all, but as a first-time dad I felt a little bit out of the loop. I couldn't feed him, and that was all he was interested in. It seemed to me that he always cried when I held him and was comforted when my wife took him. Then one afternoon, when my wife had to go somewhere, I was left alone with him. He must have been about two or three months old. I was panicked, but we did okay. I realized he actually had something to say—and he was not afraid to let me know when he liked something or when he was unhappy. It made me feel better

to realize that he was more than an eat and sleep and poop
machine. Does this sound dumb? I'm just being honest. It's
hard to be a dad. But I feel like Harry told me how to do it,
once I finally learned to listen to him. He seemed to know
more about what was required than I did.

—Darren, twenty-eight, father
of two girls and a boy, recalling
the birth of his first child

WHEN A BABY IS BORN, PARENTS CAN EASILY BECOME SO CAUGHT
up in the details of managing a family and adjusting to the schedule of the newborn that they end up navigating their way through
parenthood on autopilot, unaware of how or why they do things.
As a result, their way of parenting may come from unexamined
feelings and attitudes that they've developed over the years. *(Big*
boys don't cry. Spare the rod, spoil the child. Nice people don't get
angry.) Acting on such feelings and attitudes, without being consciously aware of what they are and how they may affect a child,
can have unforeseen consequences to both the baby's emerging
personality and the parents' own well-being.

It may be helpful to be aware that you bring a variety of
conscious and unconscious ideas, hopes, and fears to your
interaction with your baby. Your basic personality and temperament influence how you react to and handle the challenges
and responsibilities of being a new parent: Are you easygoing,
trusting, depressed, shy, impulsive, somber, affectionate, rigid,
angry, or calm? In addition, how you were brought up will have a
huge influence on how you interact with your child: Were you
treated with warmth and affection or were your parents mean

or cold? Are you determined to raise your children very differently than you were raised or are you in sync with what your parents did? In a sense, many different people and memories impact the interaction between mother, father, and baby. The significance of this process was conveyed years ago in a well-known article with the wonderful title, "Ghosts in the Nursery," by clinician and infant researcher Selma Fraiberg.

Becoming aware of these forces within you and how they affect your infant helps make you a smart parent, one who can tune in to your child's needs and individual characteristics. Your child has a great deal of potential to become a remarkable and delightful being, in charge of his or her own destiny. You can do a great deal to help make that happen.

Parents also need to realize that they themselves will grow and change in many subtle and profound ways through the experience of being a parent. Folks who are willing to think about what parenting means to them can end up being happier parents with happier kids. They don't have more predictable or orderly lives. But most of the time the parents will be able to

What Is the Parenting Autopilot?

The "parent autopilot" is a part of your personality that is assembled from:

- your own lifelong experiences as a child (that's right, not just how your parents were when you were young, but how they treat you now, too)
- your expectations and fantasies about what makes a good mom and dad
- your expectations and fantasies about what makes a good child
- your own temperament and personality

These experiences, assumptions, expectations, and fantasies blend together to shape how you act toward and react to your child. When unexamined, they shape your behavior "automatically."

handle whatever is thrown at them. They are better prepared to act in a way that benefits the child, themselves, and the family as a whole. Many years ago, the psychoanalyst Therese Benedek wrote a wonderful article, "Parenthood as a developmental phase," and Hal Hurn, another analyst, focused on the impact of the child specifically upon the father. So as you try to become ever more alert to your child's developmental stages and your role in helping baby grow and thrive, also take time to notice your many changes and challenges.

Several years ago, I had a patient whom I'll call Susan who was thirty-eight years old. Her father was an unhappy man, filled with anxiety and frequently ill with severe headaches and undiagnosed maladies. He treated Susan with indifference, because all he really thought about was himself and his problems. He was self-absorbed and wracked with self-doubt. Nothing ever seemed to go well for him; he changed jobs frequently. Although her mother was loving, it did nothing to dim the effect the father's personality had on Susan and her attitude toward men. Now, years later, Susan had her third child, a son.

Unlike her two girls, the boy was fussy and difficult. "He just doesn't seem to feel comfortable in my arms," Susan would report. But watching mother and son interact over a period of months I began to notice that it was Susan who was not comfortable with the boy. Susan would be mortified and angry to hear anyone suggest that she was less loving, more impatient, and less gentle with her son than with her daughters. But she was. When he cried she didn't rush to comfort him, as she had with the girls. She touched him less; picked him up less. "He's going to be a tough little guy, if I have anything to do with it," she said, never hearing the assumptions and attitudes that were implied through her behavior and in her words.

Susan had formed the unconscious assumption that her son would be a hypochondriac like her father; she assumed that any of his expressions of distress were just the first step down that road to becoming the kind of man she disliked—a man like her father. Determined not to indulge that, she neglected her son's expressions in order to toughen him up. Ironically, her response had the opposite effect. Inadvertently, she was setting the stage for her son to become sullen, angry, and, possibly, depressed. By not giving him the direct loving responses to his signals that he deserved, Susan was creating the very character traits in her son that she so disliked in her father.

This may sound oversimplified, but I assure you that Susan's response was neither unusual nor a sign that she was a terrible person or mother. She was simply caught up in the tangle of emotions and assumptions that shaped her personality and behavior. Unfortunately, because she had never taken the time to reflect on her attitudes toward her male child and toward child rearing in general, she was not able to tone down her least nurturing impulses and strengthen her best ones.

Parents can benefit from thinking seriously about parenting—before the baby is born, during pregnancy, after the child is born, and for the rest of the child's life to one degree or another. That's part of the bargain you make when you are blessed with a child: You get a child and in return you have to think about what being a parent means and how you act as a parent. To help you become a more self-aware parent, it may be helpful to think about the following topics. Whenever possible, you might discuss these with your partner so you both have the opportunity to increase your awareness of child-rearing issues.

TOPIC #1
Reflect on Your Own Childhood.
The ways you respond to children are influenced in part by conscious and unconscious patterns from your own childhood.

Becoming aware of those memories and the feelings they evoke will help you understand and perhaps change the way you act and react to your child.

Take time, alone and with your partner or friends, to ask yourself: What did I like about how I was raised? What didn't I like? What would I do differently? What would I do the same?

Then ask yourself specifically how your parents responded to your signals of distress, anger, fear, disgust and aversion to tastes or smells, fun, enjoyment, interest, and surprise. Take anger, for example: Did your parents restrict it, ignore it, displace it, increase it, respond to anger with anger?

When Frank and Joan tried this exercise they stumbled over some pretty surprising revelations: "I asked my husband Frank to tell me what he didn't like about how his parents raised him," said Joan, the mother of two boys, six months and five years old. "He's a very loyal son and it wasn't easy for him to talk about it, but I thought it would help us. We had had a difficult time when our oldest was a baby. Frank was working all the time and when he came home he wasn't very patient with the upheaval in the house. He would get angry when the baby cried or made a mess or interrupted him. He wasn't really mean or anything, but it made me feel like he was criticizing me and it kept him from having a good time with the baby. It's started happening again with this youngest child. When you mentioned this exercise to me, I thought we could give it a try."

Joan reported that for a few weeks Frank seemed unwilling to really answer the question. When she pushed, he talked about how his parents did the best they could in difficult circumstances. They had lived with his mom's parents when he was born and no one had a lot of privacy.

"One day, I asked him how the adults got along and how they treated him," Joan noted.

"I'd never really thought about it in those terms," Frank says now. "I mean, I was just a kid and I accepted what was around me. I knew my folks loved me and I never looked past that, I guess. But now that you ask, well, my grandfather was a very stern man, and he demanded that his house be run on his timetable and to suit his needs. When I interfered—left my toys around, cried, and threw my food—he would send me out of the room. A year old and my mom would have to take me into the bedroom, even if it was dinnertime. That punished her too. I did grow up feeling like my parents never protected me or stood up for me. No one would take my side. It's funny, but despite that I always was determined to run my house like Gramps did . . . but even more effectively. I mean, I figure if that's what they thought was good for me, then it must be good for my kids too, even if they react—as I did—by being even more wild and irritating. I guess I'm determined to prove that they did good by me. But maybe they didn't. Now that you ask me like this, I get to wondering if they weren't a little unfair to me. And am I unfair to my kids, too?"

It may take a couple of months of tossing around the subject before either parent can really get down to talking about their innermost feelings about how they were raised. Joan was smart to let it go slowly. This kind of self-reflection is best at its own pace. The results can be very revealing and may even change the way a parent relates to his or her child. And even if you or your spouse don't get around to talking out loud about such subjects, you can think this through privately and come up with some important insights into how you feel about raising your kids.

TOPIC #2
It's Your Turn to Offer Advice.
It's often easier to give advice than take it. So for this exercise, imagine that a couple has asked you for guidance on how to

become better parents. What would you tell them and what would you want them to ask themselves?

We all have a lot more to say about how other people raise their kids than how we do ourselves. It's just a lot easier to look at others than to turn the spotlight on ourselves. Sarah is a single mother: "My advice would be simple. Be prepared for how much time and attention and work it is to raise a child well. It's not something that you can really do alone. You need help; emotional support for yourself. Advice. Someone to share the responsibilities. Find a way to build a support network or you'll lose your mind. If you are married, be sure that your spouse is going to be actively involved. I see friends who might as well be single moms for all the support and involvement they get from their husbands. In some ways it's easier to be single—you aren't constantly disappointed and frustrated. I went back to my hometown to live near my mom for the first year or so of Chelley's life. I'm back in the big city now, but I couldn't have done it without Mom's help."

David, the father of a grown son and a daughter who is fourteen years younger, has another perspective. "Treat your infant like a whole person. Kids aren't stupid or oblivious. Baby talk drives me crazy. Talk to the child like they have a brain in their head and they will have stronger interpersonal and learning skills. I have friends who don't really talk to their child. I think it is because they don't think it makes a difference. But it does. To the parents too. If you don't talk to your child using an adult vocabulary, you begin to feel like your own brain is going to mush."

TOPIC #3
Ask Yourself: When You Were a Child, What Advice Would You Like to Have Given Your Own Parents?
What would you like your parents to have done differently about raising you? What do you like that they did?

Marsha was very blunt when asked this question, so blunt that she even surprised herself. "I hated it when my parents spanked me. They only used their hands, and swatted our bottoms, but it really hurt. They did it to us from a very young age. I mean, I can remember being two, so I bet they did it when we were even younger. Well, I'd pull all the typical kid stuff to thwart it—put padding in my pants, hide, throw a fit—but they were unswayed. It finally stopped when I was about ten. My mom was trying to spank me for something, I don't think it was anything too terrible, probably just sassing her. Well, I grabbed on to the leg of the dining room table and wouldn't let go. She pulled me and the table all over the room trying to shake me loose, but I was not going to give up. Finally, after she had practically destroyed the room, messing up the rug, turning over chairs, she gave up in disgust. And she never tried it again. I must say that I felt gloriously superior that day. But, in some weird way, I don't think our relationship ever recovered. We've always been very wary around one another. And that whole spanking thing is part of it somehow, I just know it. I turned out okay, and some credit goes to my mom, but much of it is just mine. I did okay *despite* a lot of the ways I was raised."

If you are uncomfortable criticizing your folks about how they raised you, it may be because you are hesitant to fault them for some of your own shortcomings. But you don't want to overlook the credit you deserve for your own personal achievements, perhaps in spite of some of the ways you were raised. You may also feel uncomfortable criticizing your parents because it feels disloyal or unkind, but having objections to certain specifics about how your parents treated you does not in any way discount their strengths and virtues as parents or people. We are all complex beings who exhibit qualities that are both admirable and objectionable.

TOPIC #4
Ask Yourself Why You Want Children.
Or ask why you want more children. Take time to think about what you expect your children to provide for you. Companionship? Help in your old age? Reflected glory? Prestige? Fun? A fuller sense of family and security? Love? Someone to need you? Do you want to have a boy, or a girl? Or do you want to provide grandchildren for your parents and get their approval yourself?

You might not be consciously aware of some of your motives for having children or having more children. However, if you can identify to some extent what functions you want your children to fulfill, you will be better able to avoid burdening them psychologically, and the long-term outcome will be better for everybody.

The urge to have a child is a powerful force and people have children for many reasons, logical or emotional, virtuous or self-centered—it's part of human nature to be driven by a swirling vortex of impulses and ideas. But at the same time it is important to become aware of your motives as much as possible; they can color your way of dealing with a baby day in and day out.

For example, parents may get in trouble when their unacknowledged motive for having a child is thwarted by the child's personality or behavior. A colicky baby is hardly going to fulfill a fantasy of having an infant who stars in commercials (and reflects her glory on you). A child with health problems may loom as a disappointment as much as a genuine worry. And an independent child may quickly destroy fantasies of having a companion who will stick by your side. Recognizing your fantasies allows you to handle whatever reality dishes up to you with less disappointment or anger. Your fantasies won't disappear, but you will be less likely to make your child an innocent victim of them.

When we asked parents about why they wanted children, they gave these responses:

- "To make life complete. Family is what life is all about."
- "Without kids you don't have a base. It's what tells you you're alive."
- "To take over the family business."
- "To do a better job than my mother did with me. To prove I can do it right."
- "For fun. Kids are a lot of fun."
- "So I won't be lonely when I am old."
- "To carry on the family name and traditions."
- "To give life a sense of purpose. Without kids you never really grow up."
- "What a stupid question. You have kids because that's the way life works."

Some of these answers are full of hope and aspiration and hold deep meaning for the parent. Others are more pragmatic. But each answer reveals an attitude that may trigger frustration or disappointment if the child doesn't live up to the expectations. The smart parent is willing to embrace the notion that a child may turn out to provide a whole set of unexpected benefits and/or problems.

TOPIC #5
Explore Your Fantasies About What Your Child Is Going to Be Like.
Take some time to think about what you imagine your child will become. A model? A doctor? A math genius? A major league ballplayer? A truck driver? Quiet? Funny? Handsome? The first woman president? A couch potato with no future?

Notice if your fantasies are positive or negative. Do they have much to do with the child or are they projections of what you'd like to become or even of what your parents fantasized about you when you were an infant?

Think about the positive and negative expectations that were placed on you as a child.

Ask yourself if your fantasies about your child come from your own fears of failure or disappointment.

Do you imagine your child's accomplishments will exceed your own? Is this pleasing or threatening?

Do you feel that you have to do and be better than your child?

It is not so easy to come to grips with what you really hope and fear for your child. Admitting disappointment and worries is tough; it can make you feel guilty, angry, scared. "My daughter Martha wasn't any more than three months old when I began to feel that I was losing control of the situation," recalls Anne, mother of now-three-year-old Martha. "I had been so sure of what my life with a new baby would be like—how perfectly wonderful, filled with pleasure, even peaceful. In fact, that was what I thought it *should* be like. To me, anything else was simply a matter of sloppy parenting. But that attitude didn't leave any room for a fussy baby or difficult breast-feeding, or family upheaval (my husband lost his job). I mean, I'm smart enough, and always thought of myself as practical, but when it came to becoming a parent, reality was not even a visitor. I don't know what I was thinking. All I know is that when life with the baby turned out to be chaotic, and not very pretty, I was devastated. I thought I was a complete failure and, how I hate to admit it, I was mad at little Martha. I became impatient with everything! If she fussed while she was feeding, or, as she got older, threw her food around when she ate, it made me angry. I felt like she was rejecting me and so I rejected her. I missed the joy of watching her discover the world day by day because I felt like she wasn't doing it right and neither was I."

Anne's clash between the reality of having Martha and her fantasies about what it would be like is not uncommon. Parents also get into trouble years down the road when they fantasize about what their child will be like as a teenager or young adult; that may be even more unpredictable than imagining what an infant will be like!

Being curious about what parents dream as to their children's future, we asked ten new parents what they wanted their children to be like as grown-ups. Several said that they wanted to have a good relationship with their child when they became elderly and needed help. They felt that it was important to have their child's friendship. Many spoke about their distance from their own parents—their feelings of love and duty but not affection. One thirty-nine-year-old single mother said: "I figure my child will be the person I love most in the world. Wouldn't it be horrible if he didn't like me and I felt all that love?"

A fifty-five-year-old businessman, starting his second family, said "I didn't get to see my kids grow up the first time. I was on the road working all the time. We have a certain family feeling between us, but we have never been real close and I think that's a shame. With this child, I'm going to do it right."

A twenty-six-year-old working mother with one daughter said: "I don't really like my folks. I don't want to have a child who feels that way about me. I am going to make sure that we are friends and that she can always trust me."

Seven parents said they wanted their child to be wealthy, or at least not to have to worry about money. Anxiety about financial security and an intense focus on status seemed to motivate these parents in part. For daughters, these parents hoped that the girls would both marry well and have successful careers in their own right.

Another group of six parents told me they wanted their children to be healthy and well liked. These are simple, basic human wishes for all children. They do not seem to have any hidden complication—except perhaps one. If being well liked becomes too overwhelming a mandate, a child may grow up to feel that expressing disagreement or legitimate anger is neither healthy nor positive. And that leads to all sorts of potential problems in self-esteem and in behavior.

Two parents said they hoped their child would be more confident and self-assured than they had been. "I was so shy. All through school, I couldn't talk in class. I was always so embarrassed. I don't know why. I was smart and pretty, but I was so anxious all the time," said one mom of a high-energy, fearless eighteen-month-old-boy. "I was determined to raise a child who felt comfortable in the world and I think I'm doing it.

"To me the big difference between how my parents raised me and how I'm raising my son is that I pay attention to what he has to tell me. My folks thought we should shut up and sit down. That was about as much advice as we ever got. There were seven of us in nine years, so I do sympathize. But if you are going to have that many kids then you better be prepared to handle it. My folks were not."

Three parents said they wanted their child to have the same profession as they did, or to go into the family business. "I run a real estate company," said one forty-five-year-old father of an infant son and a five-year-old girl. "It's my dream that when he gets through college, Steven will come and be my partner. I want to leave this business to the family for generations to come." When asked what he would do if his son turned out to want to be a teacher, or a painter or a stockbroker, he shuddered. "I'll train him from the start, take him with me to the office, help him learn as he grows up. It'll be in his blood, I know it." And if his daughter wanted to join him? "I'll cross that bridge when I come to it," he said.

One dad said he wanted his daughter to be the first woman president. "She's so great already at nine months, I just know she will be able to conquer the world."

What these parents told us is revealing, but most of their hopes and fears are pretty conscious—they didn't reveal any deep dark secrets. That takes a little more self-examination. You may want to try to bring your hidden thoughts and unconscious feelings up to the surface. This is best accomplished slowly over time or through therapy. But if you decide not to go that route, it is very helpful to see what pops out of your mouth when you answer the question: What is your most passionate hope for your child?

TOPIC #6
Discuss with Your Partner How You Are Going to Raise Your Child.

It's uncanny how many parents don't take the time to discuss their approaches to child rearing. Although many of the issues are hard to really focus on before the child actually arrives, there are some general topics, such as discipline or how you will share child-care duties, that you might want to discuss even before you become pregnant.

In general, understanding the concept of the nine signals will help a great deal in the discussion. Issues of how to treat and react to baby are resolved when you both understand why baby acts as he does and what are appropriate responses. I once saw a couple that were having terrible conflicts about getting their baby's room organized before the birth. The mom was eager to set up the room and make sure it was pretty and comfortable for the baby. Her husband thought it was ridiculous to spend the time and money when the child, in his words, "wouldn't have a clue about what the room was like anyway." In our discussions it turned out that he really didn't understand that babies react to and are affected by their surroundings. He thought of a baby as a kind of blob and didn't have much concern about how it felt or what went on around it. He also missed the fact that his wife's mood was going to be important to the baby, and if the room also made her happy that was a good reason to have the room as she wanted. It was after many hours of discussion that he gradually began to understand how responsive and communicative a newborn is and that he would play an important role in the development of his child, if he were only willing to learn.

Other topics that may be helpful to discuss include: how much time you expect each other to put into child-rearing duties; discipline; what you imagine your daily schedule will be like; issues around sleep schedules; how the house looks; schooling; child-care help; use of money; eating habits and schedules.

It can be helpful to sort these differences out ahead of time. "Marcus and I haven't really talked about the specifics of raising a child," confesses Lisa. "I got pregnant before we were married and we hadn't planned on having a child or getting married at that time, although we both wanted to at some point—and with each other. Then the baby was there and we were scrambling to make everything work out okay. Now as the baby is turning into a willful two-year-old we are finding out that we have very different ways of handling conflicts and discipline. Marcus is such a soft touch. And I believe that you have to give a kid rules and stick to them. I end up being the bad cop all the time and I resent it. But if I didn't do it, no one would. Oh, I don't know, maybe he's right. Maybe I get too punitive. But I'm beside myself. I know these differences need some discussion."

TOPIC #7
Learn as Much as Possible About
Infant and Child Development.

Understanding your infant's and child's signals and the importance and meaning of behaviors will help you become a more responsive and easygoing parent. Without outside advice or information, your parenting style may be confined to a closed system based entirely in your own upbringing and your own fantasies. You want to open up the system as much as possible. If two heads are better than one, three are better than two. When it comes to kids, it does take a library and a constant conversation with your partner, your friends, and your own inner infant.

Of course, the real key is to love your baby unequivocally—show him or her as much love and affection as possible, whether you are mother or father, whether the baby is boy or girl. However, it's not always that easy. Some people have a greater or lesser capacity to love, often based on their own upbringing. Thus, while some parents have overwhelmingly positive feelings toward their baby, others can't help but feel a lot of negative feelings. And all parents at some time will have negative feelings toward their child. Understanding the nature of your child's signals and how you interact with the child can help you have a better relationship with your infant and avoid those vicious cycles of misunderstanding in which depression, sullenness, and resentment can escalate and damage both the parent-child and the parent-parent relationship.

... And Becoming a Clued-In Parent:
Getting to Know Your Child

Just recently I missed a communication from Sarah because I just didn't see it from her point of view. The other day we were in a diner having lunch with two other friends. I put her into a seat that hooks over the table edge and slides in. She seemed to like it. In fact the whole experience was delightful. She loves to watch people and see new things and there was a lot going on in this place. So she wasn't fussy or anything. It was just that over and over she kept leaning to the far side of her seat and looking under the tabletop with this expression of great interest and bewilderment. We had been feeding her some bites of chicken and vegetables and I couldn't see over her at all—she was on the inside of a booth—but I assumed she kept dropping food down there and was peering at it. We'd say, "It's okay, here's another

*piece," or "Well, you can't have that anymore. It's on the
floor." As lunch went on she got more and more fixated on
looking down to her left. We just sort of ignored it. She
wasn't fussing. After about forty minutes we are getting
ready to leave and I go to pull the seat back so I can remove
her and it turns out that she's managed to stick her leg
between two parts of the seat where it doesn't belong and it
is stuck there against the hard metal. I couldn't believe it.
All that time she had been looking down at her leg to tell us
that something was wrong. Because it was crowded and difficult for all of us to move around and she wasn't fussing, I
never took the time to stop, to make an effort to look long
and hard at what was attracting her interest, and then help
her out. I mean really! I felt so bad. But now I know she's
not a complainer; she simply says what needs to be said and
expects that sooner or later some slow-witted adult will figure it out. I will pay a lot more attention from now on and
take the time to stop and look at what's going on from her
perspective.*

—Lynn, mother of fourteen-
month-old Sarah

ONCE YOU BEGIN TO UNDERSTAND YOUR OWN FEELINGS ABOUT
parenting, and can try to understand what your baby is "saying"
when he or she cries, coos, gurgles, and makes funny faces, you
are well on your way to creating a rewarding relationship and a

happy child. You've turned off the parenting autopilot and you're ready to fine-tune your interaction with your infant.

Seeing the World from Baby's Point of View

In any important relationship, it is helpful to understand the other person from his point of view—not yours. This is as true with an infant as an adult. If you think about your child's personality and needs, you can create an environment that allows her to grow into her best self. It's quite challenging forming deep, new relationships, and it takes time and work whether they are with colleagues, romantic partners, or small children.

Using Floor Time. One of the most effective ways to learn to see the world from your child's point of view—and to form a warm bond—is to participate in regular "floor time" together.

For at least fifteen minutes a day, or a bit longer or more often if possible, you may want to get onto the floor with your child and allow the child to direct the activities. Your role is as participant, enricher, and observer. Resist the urge to take over or be the boss. This is time for your child to tell you what she wants to do; what interests her; what she feels.

The technique was originated by Stanley I. Greenspan, M.D., Clinical Professor of Psychiatry, Behavioral Sciences, and Pediatrics at Georgetown University Medical School, and former director of the National Institutes of Health's Clinical Infant Development Program. "Floor time is a warm and intimate way of relating to a child," he says. "It means engaging, respecting and getting in tune with the child in order to help the child express through gestures, words, and pretend play what is on the child's mind. This enhances the child's self-esteem and ability to be assertive, and gives the child a feeling that 'I can have an impact on the world.' As you support the child's play, the child benefits from experiencing a sense of warmth, connectedness and being understood."

How to Make Floor Time Work. Find a comfortable spot for both of you, perhaps on a blanket, and seed it with your child's favorite toys, books, and objects. Place the child in the center of the space and get down on your stomach or sit facing the child. Get child-sized.

Follow your child's lead and join in whatever she is doing. Respond to what your child does as if it were intentional and full of meaning. Help your child do what she wants to do. Don't take over, but be a cheerful, accommodating assistant.

Once you let your child set the agenda and direct the activities, you might expand on the activities by expressing your support of her and stimulate her brain to understand the connection between her thoughts and her actions. ("That's a good girl. Are you rolling the ball to me?") Narration of activities helps your child learn how to express her own ideas and to define what she is doing for herself. But you want to be careful about how you ask questions. The phrase, "Why are you making such a mess?" is critical and unproductive. "Isn't it fun to see how far you can throw the ball?" is constructive and shows the child you understand that her actions have positive meaning. Try not to interrupt any activity; make it interactive.

Give your preverbal child a chance to answer you when you ask questions or make comments. Let her make noises, gestures, and expressions. Observe them and then respond to their messages. Remember, the child is in the driver's seat.

If your child resists your participation, don't withdraw, simply take a few seconds to see what develops and then reengage your child in play. Floor time is important because it allows your child to express herself and her interests to you, the parent. In the process it gives you the opportunity to learn about the child, and the child time to learn about herself. The interaction also sets the stage for negotiations between child and parent in times when your child wants one thing and you have a different view or agenda. Negotiation can and should take place, and what you learn about each other when your child is young will give you a firm basis for a mutually respectful relationship during the years to come.

Spending Quantity Time—Even
If the Quality Is Less Than Perfect

For a couple of decades the notion of quality time has been tossed around. Advocates have told us that even if you don't have many actual minutes or hours to spend with your kids, the time you do have will more than compensate if it is filled with particularly fabulous activities and interchanges. This whole notion was constructed to make working parents feel less conflicted and less guilty about having to divide their time and attention between children and the job. But the concept may be an essentially false construct and one that does neither children nor parents much good in the long run.

Kids need both quality and quantity time with you. And it can be all mixed up between time spent one on one, time spent within the sound of each other's voice, time spent with parent and child close to one another but each absorbed in their own activities. Time doing dull everyday tasks, time doing special fun treats, time sitting quietly, time full of activity. It's the ebb and flow of daily life and the secure, regular interplay of parent and child that form a sense of security, of knowledge of one another, and trust. Parents don't have to make every encounter with their children an "enriching" one. The pressure to make sure quality is happening may make parents act more like distant and indulgent relatives or supercharged social directors than loving parents. Sometimes less quality and more quantity is better for parent and child. And quantity time is more easily managed if you keep in mind the basic guidelines for handling infant communication—maximize interest and enjoyment, and allow expression of distress and other so-called negative signals, while responding appropriately to remove the upsetting triggers.

It's not as difficult to achieve as you may think. In the 1800s and early 1900s many people worked ten-to-twelve-hour days or longer, often with their older children alongside in the fields or factories. Today children are spared child labor in the United States and parents don't usually have to work such long hours. Most families have holiday and vacation time together—another relatively modern situation. And weekends are spent with most families based in the house together. You may not have a lot of time to take your children to great events, but there are many opportunities—laundry, shopping, mealtimes, yard work, house cleaning, reading, family hikes—to spend time together. Infants and toddlers are happy to have you nearby, talking to them, explaining what you're doing, letting them get involved one way or another. These moments of living also provide great teaching opportunities. Kids see how you think, regulate tension, and solve problems, and they internalize these patterns and make them their own.

Slowing Down

Another way to get to know your child better is to slow down. Your adult tempo may be pretty fast and you may miss what's going on in your child's mind if you simply execute a task at hand with as much efficiency and dispatch as possible and then move on to the next one. If it is hard for you to slow down, take a deep breath or two or count to ten to adjust your speedometer. This notion is related to the idea of floor time—only instead of participating in the child's play you are adapting to the child's tempo while doing "tasks" and "things that have to get done."

Tips on Baby Time

- Move slowly and calmly.
- Talk normally, put words to actions and feelings (yours and your child's), and listen.
- Follow your child's lead: How quickly (or slowly) does she like to have her pajamas put on? You might want to let her look around for a couple of seconds or minutes between putting one arm in and then the other. Play music and sing along with her as you change her diaper or say in words exactly what you are doing as you do it. Pay attention to the signals she gives you about her sense of timing and try to adopt that rhythm. You'll be surprised that it doesn't really add minutes to the overall task because minutes spent following your child's lead can prevent fussing, crying, and resisting being put in bed, which is what may happen if you rush the process.

Remember, from a child's point of view, it's difficult to be without the ability to move independently or control your environment. Infants are dependent on someone else to do almost everything. If you see the world from that point of view, you may appreciate a little more easily how upsetting it can be when someone is rushing around making you put your arms and legs into your pj's.

Reading to Infants

Even a four-month-old child can enjoy being read to: the singsong of your voice, the bright colored pictures, the secure comfort of sitting on your lap are all inviting. If you start the habit early, you offer your child yet another way to learn about using words to express emotions and ideas in place of acting out. Reading also reinforces the notion of putting ideas, thoughts, and feelings into words. Anything that enhances this process—using words—allows the child to develop more symbolic thought and creates more emotional and behavioral options for the child.

In addition, children who are read to from an early age tend to learn to read more easily, and are more ardent readers throughout their lives. And reading skills are related directly to achievement in school and life.

Also, reading to and with your child teaches you a lot about your child's personality. Children's reactions to books are vivid. They love to touch the pictures when you say the words; they laugh, get excited, flip the pages. You can get a sense of what interests and excites them. You have an opportunity to see how their minds work.

Making the World a Welcoming Place

A parent can do a great deal to make the child's world a place that feels welcoming, rather than hostile. If you are reasonably responsive to your infant's needs you create a welcoming internal world, and that helps the child see the outside world as welcoming, too. By providing a responsive, empathic environment, you help your child become optimistic and buoyant. That in turn makes the child feel confident about his ability to realistically understand the problems in the world at large.

Trying to "toughen up" your child by "not giving into his demands" or "not sympathizing with his fears" will in fact make him see the world as a scary place. That fear will constrict the child's emotional and intellectual development and make him less able to adapt to circumstances. If your child sees the world as a hostile place in which his needs will not be addressed, he may adopt an avoidant or hostile aggressive response to situations he encounters. And these responses can be limiting. The child will become weaker, not stronger. The best way to create a resilient kid—one who can handle adversity—is to provide a reasonably empathic and responsive environment. In other words, the key to getting along in the modern world is the capacity to adapt, to clearly see what is being thrown at you, whether positive or negative. Interacting reasonably and cooperatively with many types of people and situations will help your child bloom.

Guidelines, *Not* Rules

We are now going to move into the second part of the book where we look at each of the nine signals in depth. But I want to take a moment to assure you that there are many ways to raise a child well. There is no one right way, but it can really help to know about signals and how a child's inner emotional life works. This is not all about finding ironclad solutions. It is about being able to take some control over the process of parenting. Understanding the signals will give you a powerful tool for sorting out the many higgledy-piggledy events and emotions that arise from day to day.

The goal is not to be the perfect parent—there is no such thing. It is:

- to express your love and respect for your child (and yourself)
- to help your child develop tension regulation and self-esteem
- to open up communication between you and your child based on your knowledge of the nine signals . . . and to be comfortable communicating with your child in this fleeting but important time before there are words

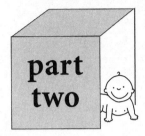

part two

The Signals

We have explored the way in which the nine inborn signals express a child's most essential needs and wants—that is, his or her earliest feelings. Now we are going to look at each signal in depth.

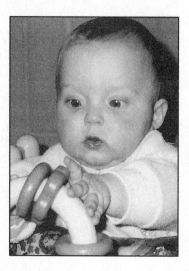

Interest

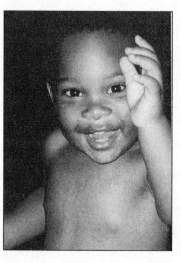

Enjoyment

Surprise

Signals of Fun:
Interest, Enjoyment, Surprise

*Normal affect development does not occur when the parents
are unable to read the emotional cues of the infant.*

—Taylor, Bagby, and Parker,
Disorders of Affect Regulation

Interest, enjoyment, and *surprise,* the three signals of fun, are
expressions of a baby's appetite for all the wonderful wealth of
information and input that surrounds him in his new world.

Two signals, interest and enjoyment, communicate a child's
delight at encountering the world and are essential to a child's
intellectual and emotional development. When parents and caregivers encourage the expression of these signals, they help the
child develop a solid emotional foundation. This enhances the
child's potential to grow into a confident, intelligent being, full of
optimism and buoyancy, ready to take on the complex and difficult challenges of life.

Surprise, the third signal of fun, is a reaction to a rapidly

occurring stimulus, such as a sudden loud noise. Surprise alerts
the baby and gets her ready for whatever may come next.

The rule of thumb is to maximize these positive signals.

- Interest and enjoyment should be encouraged,
  not squelched.
- Surprise should be handled in such a way
  that it allows the child to move from surprise
  toward interest instead of moving from
  surprise toward fear.

Interest

It is interest... which is primary.... [Interest] supports both what is necessary for life and what is possible....

—Silvan Tomkins, *Affect Imagery Consciousness, Vol. I*

When your baby expresses the signal for interest, he is clearly engrossed. His eyebrows are slightly lifted or slightly lowered. His mouth may be a bit open. If the object that's caught his attention is moving, he's following it closely with his eyes. His whole body seems alert, a little tense. He may turn his head, and perhaps his body, toward the object of interest. If he can crawl or walk, he'll move toward it. Interest is expressed on a continuum from interest to excitement.

I have two girls, grown now, but both of them, from the very beginning, expressed their special talents and personalities through what interested them. The youngest, who ended up going to art school, was always captivated by the color and shape of things—once she could crawl she would always make a beeline for the most colorful item in the room. And she loved to touch things, to trace their shape with her hands. From the very start we tried to put a lot of interesting visual experiences in front of her, to help her experience the world as she liked it. But my older daughter was much different. She seemed to like to figure things out, how they were put together, what people were saying, what things meant. She was much more analytical, and in some ways more observant, less of a participant. Maybe because she was my first, I wasn't as sure of how to encourage her. I would get her blocks, and other toys that she could build things with; then I'd get on a kick taking her to a lot of movies, even when she was only two. They held her attention, unlike most kids. She was more self-contained even at a young age. Well, she's an accountant, and a good one. Both my kids really enjoy the work they do. I guess we were able to let them discover their interests and then pursue them. I think if you really pay attention to babies, they will let you know a lot about what they will become as adults, and, as their caretaker, it's our job to help them get there as smoothly as possible.

—Kim, forty-seven

Interest

INFANTS' INTEREST IN WHAT'S AROUND THEM STARTS RIGHT FROM the beginning. Exploring the world is how they learn about themselves, others, and life in general. Infants are great big interest machines—devouring what comes across their line of sight, taking in every drop of input they can. From birth, a child's brain is programmed to seek out and respond to all forms of stimulation. Children are driven to use their senses to make sense of the world. They gain information and enjoyment from expressions of interest such as looking, touching, smelling, tasting, and those behaviors that many adults try to suppress, such as throwing, grabbing, and pulling. These exploratory, stimulus-seeking tendencies are very important: they are how we learn.

There are many times when children's expressions of interest strike adults as bad or risky behaviors. A mom's understandable concern about an infant's safety, or desire to eliminate some of the chaos, noise, and debris that an "interested" kid can produce, may create a conflict with the child's expression of interest. If a child's interests repeatedly are not given their due—are repressed, criticized, or thwarted—a child can be made to feel ashamed of his curious, exuberant behavior. This shame may constrict these exploratory activities and erode the development of self-esteem and a sense of competence. That doesn't mean that parents have to forgo order or rules or their need for a bit of peace and quiet, but it does mean that from day one parents face the challenge of finding ways to encourage and appreciate interest even as they redirect or shape it.

For example, if your baby crawls over to the wrapped package on the floor and starts pulling at the ribbon, your goal as an adult is somewhat complex: to prevent the package from being destroyed, but at the same time to see what's happening from the child's point of view, not just your own. Then you can resolve the conflict so that the package is preserved and the child is allowed to feel good about expressing interest.

To the infant, pulling on the ribbon unleashes a cascade of novelty and new information. The color and the texture of the ribbon are interesting. The fact that the ribbon, when pulled, gets longer, is intriguing. The baby is changing the shape of an object. It's a mystery and a pleasure. She is having an effect on the world; she is actually experiencing a bit of power, something children have very little of. She is unable to move through the world on her own, get food for herself or compete with adults. But with the ribbon, oh boy! Baby conquers world! In this little event there is, for the growing brain, a clue to what life can be like.

To her parent, the event may look much different. The child is destroying something that has value only when left intact. There's no pleasure or interest in untying the ribbon. The child is messing with the world as it is supposed to be. The parent feels challenged and even a little distressed.

See the conflict? With children, even the simplest interaction may have a larger meaning. In a circumstance such as this, how you react may have all kinds of repercussions, short term and long term. In the short term, your response to the signal for interest may impact your child's mood and yours—and influence whether you are left with a fussy, upset kid (never pleasant for you) or if the two of you will continue enjoying your interactions, as you nurture your child's curiosity. In the long term, if you don't take time to see what's happening from the child's point of view and try to respond with that in mind, you may establish a relationship with your child that is based on power conflicts—conflicts that often escalate and consolidate over the passing years. A relationship founded on "No" may become a battleground.

So what do you do when baby pulls on the ribbon? You can let her know she's done a great job, that's she's discovered a marvelous piece of information. "See how that ribbon works?" "You've really got that one by the tail, don't you?" There will be plenty of opportunities when she's older to explain that making the bow took effort, a concept she could never understand now. If there's time, and whenever possible, it's important to allow a baby her triumph.

At the same time you want to shift her attention and interest to a less problematic object. "See, if you pull on my shoelace, it comes untied, too. Let me show you." Or perhaps get another piece of ribbon and a box for her to play with. Or simply distract her. "Hey, what do you think about giving Teddy a ride on your belly? Here's Teddy. Want to say hello?" Redirection and distraction are your two primary tools and they do work. Shape interest, don't stifle it.

Dr. Virginia Demos, a marvelous integrator of clinical work and infant research, studied in depth these various exploratory activities and the parents' responses. She noted that one frequent misunderstanding involved a variety of activities commonly engaged in by infants, such as banging, throwing, mouthing, biting, pulling, picking up, and dropping. Unless performed when the child is angry, these activities are almost always in the service of exploration and play, and they are fueled by interest and enjoyment. Nevertheless, they may result in damage, loud noise, or irritating messes. A parent may fail to perceive the child's affective state of interest and the plans related to it, and instead focus exclusively on the consequences or potential consequences of the child's behavior. From this perspective, the parent may see such behavior as a hostile, destructive act by the child. This interpretation often leads to parental efforts to punish, scold, or restrict the child's activities. Thus, what began for the child as a relatively benign, interesting activity ends in a negative exchange with the caregiver. Because the child may not understand what specifically has provoked the parent's response—whether it was the affective state of interest; the banging, pulling, throwing; or the result of these actions— the consequences of this type of misunderstanding may be var-

ied. The child may reproduce the action in an effort to sort out cause-and-effect relationships. If I do this again, will I get the same rise out of mother? Or the child may gradually learn to curtail exploration and initiative because they tend to result in negative exchanges. Or the child may begin to view herself as hostile and destructive and therefore dangerous.

Interest

How to Maximize Interest

As a parent you not only want to respond appropriately to individual situations, such as the ribbon pulling, you also want to convey the message that the more interest the child expresses in the world, the better. This is the foundation of learning and of an agile mind.

1. Help your child learn how things work

You have the opportunity to turn each expression of interest into a greater lesson. Take the time to help your child discover what is hard or soft, tastes good or bad, sounds loud or quiet. Explore the world together. Remember, to a child everything is a mystery. The concept of cause and effect has to be learned. Pull on the tablecloth and the dishes fall on the floor—a simple enough idea for an adult—a wildly new idea for an infant. And one a baby cannot learn immediately. This lesson must be taught over and over, through experience. Luckily, you can (often) control whether it is learned through unfortunate disaster or example and explanation.

2. Encourage your child's emerging interests

For a child, the day's many intriguing experiences provides a foundation for future interests. So your best bet is to try to emphasize what seems to intrigue your child most; in so doing, you strengthen those budding inclinations. For example, many little children love trucks and construction sites, motors, and machinery. These machines do big things. They have big effects. They make noise. They are interesting shapes and colors. They are magic. Other infants adore music; they respond to rhythm and love to be sung to. Notice your child's favorite things and use them as learning tools. They also are very effective when you are trying to redirect or distract your child.

By tuning in to what captivates your child's attention, you are telling your child, "I get it. I see what you like and I think enough of it to share your interest and encourage it." This validates the child's interests and feelings, which in turn build a child's self-esteem and confidence.

As Virginia Demos noted, children use a variety of techniques to involve parents: they bring them objects, pull at their legs or arms, flop in their laps, ask questions, or smile at them. Even a perfunctory response from the parent is sometimes sufficient to sustain the child's interest or playfulness. But ignoring the child at such times, or reacting with irritation or prohibitions, tends to dampen the child's capacity to sustain the interest and enjoyment on his own. There are a variety of reasons for this type of parental behavior—ranging from temporary lapses due to fatigue or a preoccupation with other concerns to more characterologic factors. In the latter case, the parent might believe that child's play is silly; or feel embarrassed at playing on a child's level; or assume that as long as children don't cry or fuss a grownup need not get involved. But to the child, all these responses communicate the same thing—that her joy and and playful intentions have been perceived and understood, but they have not been accepted and supported. The lack of a positive response to expressions of interest-excitement and enjoyment may have all or some of the following meanings to the child: I am not interesting and enjoyable, it is not worthwhile to be interested and joyful; it is not worthwhile to be interested and joyful about this particular thing; I shouldn't bother trying to engage Mommy or Daddy in my interests and joys. Any one of these conclusions may inhibit the child's positive signals and create a temporary barrier to further communication with the parent. According to Tomkins's theory of affect, such a situation will evoke shame in the child. Moreover, depending on the child's response to shame, other negative affects, such as distress or anger, are likely to be added to the sequence.

3. Allow the child to fully express the signal for interest

Look at every signal of interest as an opportunity to build your child's self-confidence and brain power. If adult scissors are tempting to your thirteen-month-old, you can gently take them away and replace them with children's scissors. Then show him how to use the scissors. Take the time demonstrate how they work and how sharp they are. Let the child know you appreciate his interest in them but that you must protect him from the danger they pose. "See, you put a piece of paper into them and you can turn that piece of paper into four pieces of paper. How neat is that? But these scissors are too sharp and can hurt you, so I can't let you have them; let's try these scissors which are duller." This reasoned approach helps the child learn about scissors without suppressing the child's signal of interest or scaring the child.

Virginia Demos shed light on the problem that arises if you simply remove the scissors or yell "No"—even if your main focus is on protecting the child from harm. This response fails to support the infant's built-in urge to explore interesting objects. The opportunity to learn about scissors is lost, and no other interesting substitute is provided. The message to the infant is simply, "Stop." But, asks Demos, "Stop what?" Stop being interested? Stop exploring new objects? Stop exploring scissors? If this type of prohibition occurs frequently enough, the infant may learn to inhibit her exploratory, learning, stimulus-seeking behaviors on her own and may become increasingly constricted and immobilized.

Why "No" Can Be Heard
As a Three-Letter Word

If you frequently step on your child's expressions of interest by reprimanding her with a sharp "No!" or a "Stop that!" you may make her feel shame and humiliation. That's the natural reaction when you tell your infant that she is "wrong" for being interested in this or that object. Abruptly breaking off a child's expression of interest makes it painfully clear to the child that she can't share feelings of interest with you without being scolded.

Also, a sharp "No!" or even simply, "Don't touch that!" can be confusing for a baby. The world can be a scary place to a child and she may need reassurance to bravely go where she has not gone before. If you abruptly stop her expression of interest, she may not know what to do next. "Okay, I'll stop, but now what? What am I supposed to do?" she wonders. This shifts the signal for interest to one for distress; the child may start wailing as soon as you take the scissors away. You may think that your child's immediate distress means she is upset because she can't have what she wants. You may even say, "You spoiled little thing!" But that's not all that's going on. The shift to crying happens because the child feels acutely misunderstood. Not only was her interest interrupted, which is no fun, but it was discounted as wrong. This undermines the formation of self-esteem and confidence. In short, "No" said too often and too quickly translates in a baby's brain as "b-a-d."

Why to Maximize Interest

Clearly, signals of interest indicate that a child wants to learn about the outside world. But they also help a child learn about himself. When interest is stimulated, it shows a child what brings him pleasure, what captures his attention, what excites him.

- Encouraging interest helps your child become *confident about exploring.* It allows him to satisfy his biological needs for stimulation and tells him it's okay to expand his world without feeling guilty.
- When you reward curiosity, you strengthen a child's *sense of control, competence,* and *confidence.* He begins to sense that he can manage "out there" in the world.
- Learning that there are limits is critical too. Seeing what's allowed and what's not allowed helps the child develop an *understanding of boundaries.* Your child will be reassured to find out that there are rules and that you can be counted on to teach her what they are. This will allow your child to learn how to *self-regulate* her impulses and desires so that she can follow the rules, fit in, and gain your approval.

The Interest Timeline

All infants are interested in what they can see, hear, and touch. Initially, they use their mouths and senses of taste to assess many objects they encounter. Then, as their vision and hearing become more acute and they can move around more easily, the variety of things that spark their interest increases. Your role is to help your child find ways to express her interests and to expose her to new interactions that may stimulate new interests. Granted, it can be a hit-or-miss situation sometimes, but that's okay. For example, some children will enjoy being read to at six months, others may not get into it until they are nine months or older. Your child will let you know immediately if reading is an activity that evokes interest. If it's not a hit, she'll squirm, fuss, and shift her attention to something else. That's your signal to set it aside for the time being.

Other activities that evoke interest in infants include playing with stuffed animals, going for walks, being sung to, or shaking a rattle. No activity is too trivial or too minor where interest in concerned. If it captures your child's attention, whatever the age, go with it.

As your child grows, and her interests expand, your ability to tune in to what stimulates her curiosity may feel like it comes and goes. Don't worry, this can happen as children pass from one developmental stage to the next and their expanding interests surpass their ability to communicate them. Temporarily, the misreading of a signal can lead to heightened frustration and distress—for your child, and for you. For example, Lois told me that she was having a terrible time keeping daughter Eva, usually such a happy child, from crying. It hadn't been a problem before, but now at sixteen months, Lois felt like something was terribly wrong. After observing mom and child together over a couple weeks, I could see that the baby was frustrated by not being able to talk yet. Eva could understand what was being said to her, and she struggled to talk back using sounds and almost-words. But she couldn't yet say, "I want . . ." or "I need . . ." and the frustration was getting to her. When she became interested in something or had an opinion to express, she wasn't able to get it across quickly enough. She became impatient and fussy. To help Eva during this transition, Lois made an extra effort to put words to her child's signals and to narrate what was going on.

Sometimes parents may understand their child's interest but misunderstand their current developmental capacities and their need to have the enthusiasm and accomplishments validated—thereby puncturing the balloon of good feeling. Demos described one such situation between a mother and her fifteen-month-old daughter. The child was playing outdoors in her sandbox while her mother sat nearby in a chair. A neighbor boy had just thrown a ball to the girl in the sandbox. She picked up the ball and "threw" it back. As often happens at this age, the ball dropped about two inches in front of her. Nevertheless, she was delighted with her efforts, smiled broadly at the boy, and clapped her hands. The mother said, "You can't clap yet; the ball didn't go out of the sandbox. Try again." The girl looked a little puzzled, but she did try again, with much the same result and the same excitement and joy. The mother again insisted that the girl had not achieved "her" goal.

Interest

By the third and fourth repetitions of this sequence, the child's expression had become sober; she was no longer clapping. Indeed, she soon lost all interest in throwing the ball and turned to other objects in the sandbox. From the child's point of view, joining the game of catch and "throwing" the ball back to the boy probably meant simply moving her arm and letting go of the ball, which was as close as she could come to imitating the boy's action. Her joyful, excited response clearly indicated that, by her lights, she had succeeded. Her mother's refusal to accept her goal—to see her efforts as an achievement—and to share in her joy left the child feeling perplexed and unsupported. Not understanding how she had failed or how to succeed and please her mother, she gave up the task.

How to Tune In to
Your Child's Interests

One good way to understand just what interests your child is to use floor time (see Chapter 10). This puts you into the child's world in a way that few other activities can do. If your child crawls off into the kitchen and starts playing with the pots and pans, crawl along with her and see just how fascinating it is when you're at a kid's eye level. You will begin to appreciate how large a part the smallest encounters with outside objects play in a child's imagination. And you'll get a sense of the tempo at which your child moves through the world. Allowing kids to maintain their own sense of time is important if you are to encourage exploration and help build self-confidence.

Quantity, not just quality, time is also important. When your time with your child is too event oriented, too structured or scheduled, you don't allow your child to simply move through the day at an unforced pace, interacting with the environment in spontaneous ways. Spend time with your child as you do laundry, while you read, as you do errands or just hang out. In these ordinary circumstances, a child can express extraordinary interest, and you will have the opportunity to observe and interact with your child in an easy, natural way.

What to Do When You
Must Interrupt Interest

An important part of maximizing your child's interests is learning how to manage situations where you must interrupt the expression of interest—which frequently leads to distress and anger. For example, you are standing at the deli counter in the grocery store waiting to be served. Your child is fascinated by everything that is going on—the slicing machines, the other people, the strange-looking objects in the deli case. But once you are served, you have to finish up your shopping. As you turn to wheel your child down the next aisle, he lets out a wail that can be heard in the next county. He wants to stay right there and keep looking at all the activity. You need to keep moving. One response in such a situation is to recognize his distress and validate it: "Hey sweetie, you really liked watching all that, didn't you?" You might even wheel him back to the counter and say, "Look there's the butcher. And there's that delicious turkey you like. I know it's upsetting to have to move on, but let's see what's next."

You then can help your child learn to overcome his distress by finding something else to focus on. You may offer distraction by singing a song or offering him a toy or a favorite transitional object (his blanket or teddy). You may tell him that you are off to see just what there is to explore down the next aisle, or you can go through an elaborate goodbye ritual as you leave the butcher.

By validating your child's interest and allowing him to express his distress and then moving on to other activities, you help your child develop tension regulation and the capacity to delay gratification. You also gently make it clear that sometimes he is not the center of the world. Sometimes other people or events will prevail. Your child will feel better about that startling fact if you handle necessary interruptions of interest in ways that help him remain calm, such as providing distractions.

Early Education

Within this context of exploratory patterns and behaviors, one might ask: How important and how effective are early educational programs (such as Head Start)? The answer is that such programs are very important and potentially very effective.

However, a more important issue arises even earlier in the child's life: Do the parents understand the child's signal of interest? Understanding the interest affect means appreciating that the baby's curiosity, tendency to explore and examine, play, and "get into things" are all learning opportunities. Of course, some limit setting is necessary, and you can be creative in protecting the child from dangerous items without squashing their curiosity and enthusiasm. But try not to constrict these explorations or see them as "misbehaviors." Your child should have as much freedom to think and say and explore as possible. When words emerge (see Chapter 19, "Beyond Signals"), one can encourage the verbal expression of feelings. If your child begins using what you might consider "bad" words, use this as a learning experience. Reach for a dictionary, and talk with the child about the meaning of the word. Together, decide whether or not the word offends people, if it should be used in public, and so on. The trick is to encourage, not constrict, this kind of learning opportunity as early as possible. This approach promotes real "early education"!

The Continuum

Interest, like the other signals, is not a rigid state. It can be expressed as everything from mild curiosity to enthusiasm and excitement. When Grandma brings baby a new toy car, he may stare at it in an offhanded way, putting it down, picking it back up, not sure of what he thinks. But after a while he may decide that it is pretty wonderful and begin waving it around over his head. His interest has increased to excitement. This is getting good, he thinks. If he accidentally hits a button that activates a siren, that's surprising at first and then may be even more exciting.

Interest can decrease, as well as increase. Sometimes, a child will express initial interest in something, but then it fades. If the toy car, on closer inspection, doesn't capture his fancy, there isn't much you can do to change his mind, no matter how hard you try. If you try repeatedly to engage your child's interest in the car, you may instead provoke his anger. His tears or writhing around in your arms are his way of signaling, "Aren't you listening to me? I don't want to play with that thing." In such a situation, it's better to put the toy aside and substitute another more engaging one or to look around and see what it is that's occupying his interest. Perhaps Grandma herself is more intriguing. Let them interact and don't worry about the toy.

For kids, boredom is almost unbearable; they crave interesting interaction and grow distressed when they don't have it. That's why children can become so fussy and disruptive in restaurants or at the mall. They need a lot of toys or puzzles or other distractions in those situations to satisfy their natural, built-in, healthy curiosity and stimulus-seeking tendencies.

To recap: If you are able to help your child understand and gravitate to what interests her, you and your baby both reap great benefits now and in the future. Kids who know what they are interested in and get parental support for those interests have an easier time later on establishing a life's work that they enjoy. And that should make you feel pretty happy too.

Enjoyment

Enjoyment is signaled in various ways. The baby smiles. Her lips widen and extend up and out. She laughs and there is some wrinkling of the cheeks and brightening of the eyes. Often she makes various kinds of high-pitched sounds and gleeful noises. Enjoyment exists on a continuum from enjoyment to joy.

My mother always called me the bad child. I think it was because I was so exuberant. I've come to realize that she believed enjoyment was a little sinful. She never said it; but inside I think it's what she felt. It was how she was raised. As a result it took me years to become comfortable in the world, to have fun, to be able to be silly. Now that I have kids of my own I am so aware of that. I mean, I tell them all the time

how good they are, and I try to be as playful as possible. I
want a house filled with laughter and I have it. My two—
one's eight months and one is about twenty months—make
me laugh so often. The little one does this goofy thing when
she is delighted. She opens her eyes and mouth as wide as she
can and sticks her tongue out and then breaks into giggles.
She loves it when I do it too. It makes me feel a lot of sympa-
thy for my mom, who missed out on so much and had such
a hard time enjoying life's pleasures.

—Jane K., thirty-four,
graphic designer

ENJOYMENT IS SERIOUS STUFF. THE ABILITY TO FEEL AND EXPRESS
joy is essential to building a happy, healthy life. That's why it is
helpful to be attuned to what your child enjoys and to look for
every opportunity to help your child capture the feelings of pleasure and delight, which can be sustained after the moment's
enjoyment fades.

A child often goes back and forth between signals for interest
and enjoyment. This creates an overall sense of playfulness and
pleasure. For example, when your baby notices her favorite colorful mobile moving above the crib and hears the familiar melody
that accompanies the motion, she may coo with interest and
enjoyment. In response, you give the mobile a gentle pat to make
the motion more intriguing and you begin making funny noises
to accompany the motion of the mobile. The baby is restimulated
by your interaction with the mobile and your singing. Not only
does the baby experience these pleasurable sensations again, she

also is made to feel good because you have noticed and positively responded to her experience. Then, when you stop singing and making the mobile move, the two of you laugh. With the laugh, the baby is experiencing a genuine, though brief, sense of enjoyment and joy. But her underlying feelings of happiness and contentment remain. Enjoyment may be a fleeting sensation, but the benefits are long-lasting.

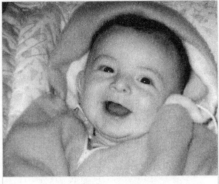

Enjoyment

Understanding the Signal for Enjoyment

Research suggests that enjoyment is triggered by a decrease in stimulation and a falloff in the accompanying neural firing in the brain. It works like this: An intense stimulation occurs. Then, as quickly, the intensity falls off. It's like when a comedian tells a joke: tension builds as the comic describes some scenario—you are provoked, or intrigued, and listen intently—then, ba-da-boom, the punch line arrives and you laugh with enjoyment.

There are various intensities of enjoyment, from a quiet smile to a loud burst of laughter, from a simple pleasure to flat-out joy. Since enjoyment is triggered by a decrease in stimulation, it often *follows* interest, surprise, or even fear—signals which depend on an increase of stimulation. Recall the relief (joy) you feel when something scary or painful stops. Or the sustaining involvement you feel after the initial sensation of joy fades when you are experiencing something of genuine interest. That's why throughout this chapter you may notice that discussions and examples of enjoyment will reveal a subtle interaction with the other signals, especially interest.

Cultivating Enjoyment

Despite the transient nature of enjoyment, it is important to recognize the signal when it occurs and to help your child find many opportunities to experience the feeling. Few things make a young child feel as good about the world and his relationship to his caretakers as sharing moments of enjoyment.

Whatever the age of your infant, you can help your child express enjoyment by recognizing what triggers it, by sharing the child's feelings. Offer your baby the chance to repeat the enjoyable experience. You might also put words and sounds to the experience to help your child learn how to express enjoyment. For example, Susan gave her daughter a music box that played the "Dance of the Sugarplum Fairies" from the *Nutcracker Suite*. When the lid to the colorful box was raised, a ballerina in a gauzy pink skirt twirled around and around. Lily, the baby, was captivated. So Susan made playing the music box a regular part of their getting-dressed routine. She'd say, "Lily, would you like to have a visit with your ballerina?" Susan would open the box, to release the music and the ballerina. Then she would take Lily's hands and conduct to the music, play patty cakes, and sing along with the tune, making up funny lyrics. Lily would make sounds of glee, clap her hands, and stare intently at the twirling figurine. Lily was learning that her mother understood and approved of what she enjoyed, and she was realizing that when she felt enjoyment she could express it through words, singing, and motion. In addition, at a time when babies can become fussy—getting a child dressed can be difficult sometimes—Lily and Susan were having fun.

As your baby gets older, you may want to make an extra effort to put words to moments of enjoyment. Don't just narrate what's going on, talk about how it makes your child feel. When baby giggles or coos, try gently talking about what you observe in your child: "You like that, don't you, sweetie?" "Does that noise make you laugh?" "Isn't it fun to see how much noise you can make?" "Aren't you proud of your discovery?" "You sure are strong, look at you lift that up over your head."

So, when your son thrills at a visit from a friendly dog, help him express his joy by saying something like, "Seeing a dog is exciting, isn't it? Don't you love how soft their coat is to touch? Do you think he'll lick your face?" If, instead, all you can do is admonish him, "Don't let that dog get his dirty germs all over you!" or "Don't touch, he might bite!" then your delighted child will become confused. His enjoyment and interest have provoked your criticism and alarm. If such incidents are repeated day in and day out in different situations, he may begin to feel that he is not entitled to feel enjoyment or that he is pretty stupid for thinking that he knows what is enjoyable.

If you find your child is expressing enjoyment about something that is potentially dangerous, you can encourage the joy and still intervene. For example, your six-month-old has gotten hold of a box of tiny buttons and is shaking it with pleasure. The box is threatening to open. Suddenly grabbing away the box will carry the message that the enjoyment of the rattling sound is not acceptable. But saying in a warm and positive voice, "What a nice sound!" and then substituting another, safer container of things that rattle (a securely fastened box of plastic checkers pieces) tells the baby that you understand how much fun he's having.

If you suspect that you may be squashing your child's moments of enjoyment, take the time to reflect on your own motivation. Why are you trampling on your child's enjoyment?

Are you afraid of the dog? Why? How can you handle your fears so that you can remain cautious without being alarming? How can you manage your worries, protect your child, and still give him the positive message that you support his feelings of enjoyment? When dealing with enjoyment, as well as the other signals, it is often wise to take time for a little self-reflection. You may find that your own anxieties, or your own difficulties with expressing enjoyment, may be interfering with how you relate to your child. Make a promise to yourself to increase your experiences of enjoyment; in fact, let your child be your guide. Look for and share his moments of enjoyment.

Simple Pleasures: Easy Ways to Stimulate Enjoyment

- Young infants love to become mobile—remember, without your intervention they are stuck in one place. Pick them up, twirl them around, raise them into the air above your head, take them for a walk in the stroller, or just walk around the house with them in your arms. Watch their delight and help them express their enjoyment enthusiastically.
- Stimulate their sensory feelings of touch, hearing, and sight—but gently and without overloading their circuits. For example, some babies respond with great pleasure to the soft feel of a stuffed animal or their favorite blanket on their cheeks. Some love to stroke the cat's back. They may also enjoy certain kinds of music, either recorded or sung to them. Kids also are thrilled with peek-a-boo or any slightly surprising visual game.
- Let your child show you what she likes. From an early age, babies have strong opinions about

what brings them enjoyment and what makes them distressed. Although you will, of course, introduce your child to all kinds of new activities and constantly be supplying her with new information about the world around her, you want to make sure you give the child enough room to express her desires, her enthusiasms, her opinions about what is fun and what is enjoyable. Always keep your eye out for the signals your child is expressing.

Enjoyment Is Also an Important Part of Playfulness

Playfulness (see Chapter 6) is the result of combining interest, enjoyment, and surprise. If your child is amused by a bouncing ball and you say "Boing, boing, boing," you are being playful. You are teaching your child that it is a good thing to relish pleasurable moments. And you are stimulating the child to move to interest in the engaging event. You may then move on to showing your child various ways to play with a ball. You have the opportunity to acknowledge your child's enjoyment and interest and sustain it. Another example: Your ten-month-old is having a wonderful time on a swing. As you gently push him forward you might say something like, "Up we go," or "Wheee!" It is important for you to connect your expression with the baby's delight at the feeling of motion. This lets the child know you share the feeling of fun and reinforces your child's positive feelings. It also reinforces the child's interest in the swing. The combination of validating enjoyment and interest in one act helps the child learn what he likes. And learning what he likes is absolutely essential for your child to grow up confident and secure.

The Enjoyment Timeline

Newborns' needs are simple and their ability to express signals, which exists from day one, is just developing. At this point, enjoyment comes from prompt attention to basic needs: clean diapers, food when hungry, sleep, a loving touch, sweet soothing words and sounds, a relatively calm, controlled environment.

As a child gets slightly older, enjoyment is associated with ever more complex stimulation. She can now see more clearly and is very tuned in to facial expressions and sounds. Enjoyment

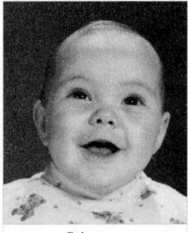

Enjoyment

comes from the basics of food and warmth and love, just like before, but now it also comes from the ability to comprehend visual and audible jokes such as peek-a-boo or funny noises. Physical sensations also add to enjoyment. As infants grow, they enjoy a careful airplane ride above your head, swinging on swings, "riding a horsey" on your knee, and raspberries on the belly.

As they near their first birthday, children may be eager to talk, they just can't yet. But you can see the urge to talk in their signals. Your steady stream of verbal communication is very important to them. Listen when they vocalize—it becomes quite elaborate, a garbled language all their own. Respond fully. Talk about what is fun or interesting or silly. Explore emotions and ideas. Your child is understanding a great deal more than you may think.

The Benefits of Cultivating Enjoyment

Enjoyment may be fleeting but it is a building block for many personality traits that are vital to creating a happy, successful life. When you elicit and encourage the signal for enjoyment you allow the reasonable expression of feelings and validate your child's perception of the world. That tells your child that the people around him understand his emotions and needs. This in turn helps the child develop a sense that the world is a friendly place in which his needs will be met and helps the child become more buoyant and optimistic. Furthermore, as baby learns more about what brings him pleasure, he is developing a positive sense of self. Your approval of his expression of enjoyment tells him you approve of his feeling. In addition, through your active participation in enjoyment, the child learns that what feels good to him is also pleasurable to you, the parent. You validate his experience and help him become aware of what he thinks and feels.

Enjoyment Helps Stimulate Intellectual Development.
Learning is stimulated when encountering the world and having varied experiences are enjoyable, not discouraging or frightening. Children who are encouraged to interact in positive ways with whatever comes their way, and who can take delight in the world around them, are much more likely to follow their interests and to feel confident about expanding their capabilities.

Expressing Enjoyment Helps Create Good Social Interaction.
Your interaction with your baby about enjoyment builds his ability to make a pleasurable connection with others. Kids who know how to enjoy themselves and express a positive outlook on the world have an easier time making a place for themselves in the social network they encounter at home, in preschool, and on

the playground. Other people will respond positively to your child's playfulness and enthusiasm.

Having a Solid Sense of Enjoyment Creates Resiliency.
Enjoyment, along with interest, is an essential element in establishing optimism, self-esteem, and confidence. When you maximize a child's positive signals—and enjoyment is indisputably positive—you help your child grow into a secure, confident person. Then when tough times come—your son is teased on the playground, your daughter has a falling out with her best friend—he or she has the reserves of confidence and security needed to bounce back from adversity.

Knowing What She Enjoys Helps Your Child Make a Satisfying Career Choice.
As your child develops, learning how to identify and express what she enjoys is an important step in becoming a mature adult who is able to pursue interests that provide stimulation, gratification, and a sense of accomplishment. It is not too much to say that the seeds of a successful career grow and blossom, in part, because of the way you respond to your child's earliest signals of enjoyment.

One More Time: Don't Worry About Spoiling Your Child

Over and over I hear parents say and do unintentionally harsh things to their infants because they are more afraid of "spoiling" their child than almost anything else. They don't want a brat who thinks the world is his oyster or that it owes him anything. The message they want to communicate is: "Be tough. Don't whine.

Don't cry. And for heaven's sake, don't think you are supposed to be happy all the time. Get real."

I want all parents to stop for a moment and think. *We are talking about infants here.* Infants cannot be given too much love, encouragement, support, attention, time, patience, love, or happiness. No such thing. The world will knock your child around plenty in a few short years. It does everyone. You don't need to throw the first metaphorical punch. The best way to prepare your child to have the strength, endurance, patience, and self-confidence to weather the hardships of growing up is to lay a foundation from day one that gives her the ability to recognize and express emotions.

Surprise

When signaling surprise, a baby's eyebrows move up, the eyes are wide open and blinking, and the mouth is in an open "o" shape. Her head may turn, and she may make an effort to turn her body if the surprise came from the side or in back of her.

Jennifer gets startled very easily. She is very sensitive to things like horns honking or doors slamming. I'd say they actually scare her. I'm hoping she'll grow out of it as she begins to realize a little more about cause and effect. But in the meantime I have decided to just try and keep her out of harm's way as much as I can. When I can't, I try to turn the whole episode into a learning adventure. Once when there was a bagpipe playing at the mall, she was really upset. The moment that sound started she jumped and scrunched up her face and looked so alarmed. I took her into a store to get away from the sound. Then when the guy took a break, I wheeled her over to him and explained that she had been really frightened and asked if she could touch the bagpipe. He then showed her how he blew on it to make a sound. She became a little more trusting and curious. I wouldn't say she was a convert really, but at least I could wheel her from store to store without her screaming in alarm if the bagpiper was playing.

—Betsy, mother of three
children, including fourteen-
month-old Jennifer

THE WORLD IS A SURPRISING PLACE, FULL OF UNEXPECTED NOISES, shapes, and happenings. For infants, more than adults, surprises

Surprise

can be bewildering. Think about how you may jump out of your skin at an unexpected loud noise; now just imagine how inexplicable it is to a baby who has no backlog of experience to measure a startling noise or event against. The immediate function of surprise is to allow us to shift our focus from what we were thinking about to something that may be a threat or that calls for our immediate attention.

Research has found that when we are surprised, our brain is overtaken with a sharp increase of brain activity. This is evolutionarily beneficial since it alerts us to potential harm from the outside. However, once surprise is felt, a child (or adult for that matter) has an equal chance of going on to experience interest or fear. Which way it goes depends on three factors. The first is the quality of the surprise itself. If the surprise is the result of a vacuum cleaner being turned on, the child's response will probably be less intense than if a whole bookcase were to fall over with a huge crash. The second factor is the response of the environment—is mom or dad calm in the face of the surprise? And third is the child's temperament and level of reactivity. Some children, like Jennifer in the story above, have more sensitive startle responses than others.

How to Regulate Surprise

Here, your goal is not to maximize the response, as with interest or enjoyment. You want to control, regulate, and reshape it so that it has the maximum benefit for the child. But you have to be prepared to react quickly! Surprise happens suddenly. The two keys to transformation of surprise into a positive signal (interest or enjoyment) are validation and action.

- Validation means that your response reassures your baby that there was indeed a surprise and that you are there to make it better by taking appropriate action. This is much more constructive than using shame—such as, "What are you? A fraidy cat?"—to manage surprise. Feeling ashamed can lead to all kinds of self-doubt and trigger an anger response.

• Action is used in two ways: Sometimes you need to
act to protect your child from the stimulation that
triggered the surprise. When a parked car's alarm
suddenly goes off as a baby is being wheeled down
the sidewalk in a stroller, the child may register
surprise that quickly moves to startle. Fear may
just be around the corner. If you bend down and
lightly cover the baby's ears, saying "Oh my, that's
so loud. We were surprised! Let's move, okay?" and
then move the stroller away from the car, your
baby will have ample opportunity to see that you
understand and will calm down. Some well-inten-
tioned parents may pat their babies on the head,
and say, "Oh, that wasn't so loud now." What happens when a parent does this? The baby isn't sure
you understand his signal of surprise and feels
unprotected and misunderstood.

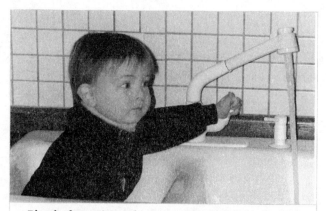

Blend of surprise and interest: This little boy climbed
into the sink and has just turned on the water,
showing a blend of surprise and interest.

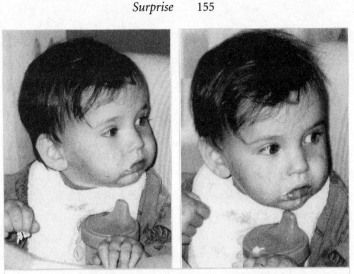

Surprise   Interest

This little boy was surprised to hear his name called suddenly
from behind him, and he shows the shift from initial surprise
to interest moments later (note the eyebrows, raised in surprise
and lower in interest).

You can also use action to respond appropriately to your
child's surprise by helping your child move from surprise to
interest. Let's say you're at the mall and a clown pops out from
behind a corner. This is supposed to provide fun and entertain-
ment for a child, but it can just as easily trigger surprise moving toward fear. It is not unusual for kids to be frightened of
clowns, and I think it is because of the distortion of the facial
features.

If you notice that your child is startled, you may want to
back off calmly and talk quietly about the clown. "He looks
strange, doesn't he? He's a clown, just a guy in a costume. Shall
we watch him?" You can hold your child in your arms while
the two of you look at and talk about the clown. Working with
your child will help transform the child's sense of surprise into a

positive experience. He will learn that such events can be worth experiencing, and, though a bit unnerving at first, might be quite intriguing.

The Benefits of Managing Surprise Wisely

When you respond quickly and appropriately to your child's surprise, you set the stage for emotional honesty. By recognizing the child's emotions and potential distress and responding in a helpful way, you encourage the child to continue to share her feelings, including her less than positive ones, with you. You also tell your child that she is worthy of protection and that you value her reaction—a direct road to self-esteem. And finally, when you help your child discover that something that was initially surprising may be interesting, you encourage openness to new things, which is a precursor to a healthy interest in learning.

Signals for Help:
Distress, Anger, Fear,
Shame, Disgust, and Dissmell

The mother functions as a container for receiving and sharing the infant's primitive sensations and emotions... [these] are transformed through the mother's cognitive processes... [and are] conveyed back to the infant (i.e., the mother functions as a thinking apparatus for the infant).

—Taylor, Bagby, and Parker,
Disorders of Affect Regulation

Signals for help are a baby's defense against harm and aid in survival. Infants have no other means of self-protection. They use these signals—distress, anger, fear, shame, and aversion to unpleasant tastes and smells—to alert their caretakers to their needs and unhappiness. Parents succeed by respecting the powerful communications that these signals transmit and responding reasonably promptly to the calls for assistance that they trumpet.

157

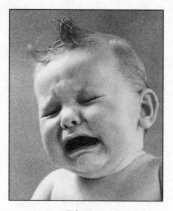

Distress

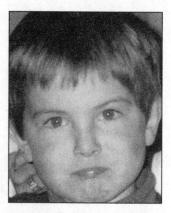

Anger

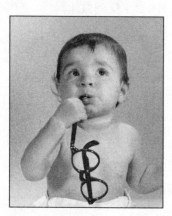

Fear

Shame

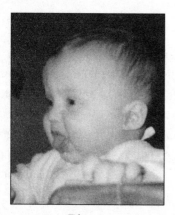

Disgust

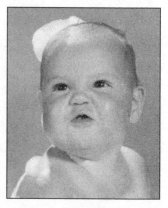

Dissmell

The key is to allow the expression of negative emotions and then attend to the triggers so the child's distress goes away. These signals for help—distress and anger, for example—are *communications*, not attacks. If parents try to stamp out these signals, a child will have a hard time expressing the signals or knowing what he really feels. If parents do not attend to a child's signals for help, the child may begin to sense that the world is a perilous place, not much interested in his needs and unresponsive to his opinions or feelings. The reasonable handling of the signals for help is crucial in order for a child to develop a sense of optimism, buoyancy, and hopefulness and to prevent the growth of feelings of depression, anger, and despair.

Distress

Distress is the affect of suffering, making the world
a vale of tears.

—Silvan Tomkins, *Affect Imagery*
Consciousness, Vol. III

The signal for distress is expressed through crying, arched
eyebrows, a turned-down mouth, tears, rhythmic sobbing,
fussiness, or withdrawal. Distress may launch older babies
into a frenzy of activity. This is revealed by a scrunched-
up face and windmilling or wiggling arms. Older children
might whine or get into everything, wreaking havoc.
Although how a child expresses distress may change as she
grows, the meaning of the signal remains the same, as does
the appropriate way to respond. This signal exists on a continuum of emotion from distress to anguish.

Sophia, our granddaughter, is generally a happy baby, thrilled with stroller rides, open and friendly to everyone she meets. Well, one day my husband and another friend and I picked her up and took her for an afternoon in the park. You could see right from the start that this little nine-month-old was having to make an effort to be sociable; she'd respond to our attention for a while and then get fussy. We fretted and talked about what it could be. We tried taking her out of the stroller and carrying her, singing songs, giving her a bottle, some graham crackers, moving slowly, moving more quickly. Nothing worked. Her nose was all scrunched up, she looked sad. She squirmed around. The collective effort of three relatively intelligent, sensitive adults could not solve the distress. After a couple of hours we were sitting on a park bench when I leaned over and pulled off her socks. My, these are tight, I thought. They had left a red elastic mark on her calves. When I took her socks off, she laughed. Actually laughed. And her distress dissolved. So don't tell me it's easy to figure out what's troubling a little one. We tried everything we could think of. It was just dumb luck that I figured it out. Deciphering what makes a baby unhappy isn't always easy.

—Katherine, fifty-two, grandmother

DISTRESS IS A USEFUL SIGNAL, COMMUNICATING IMMEDIATE NEED. It is an SOS. In small babies, it tends to be triggered by hunger, fatigue, illness, discomfort, or pain. Distress indicates that something is not right. As kids get older, it can also indicate that they are feeling bored, lonely, or sad. In addition, distress may signal that there are other powerful emotions churning in your little one. For example, when the child is feeling excessive fear or shame or disgust, he may express distress. Heightened distress may lead to anguish. Most important, with further escalation, distress can turn into anger (see Chapter 15).

When distress intensifies, parents are often troubled or irritated by what they perceive as their child's over-the-top reaction and may have trouble figuring out what happened to set it all off in the first place. It is important to remember that signals for help, such as distress, are communications, not attacks or evidence of being spoiled.

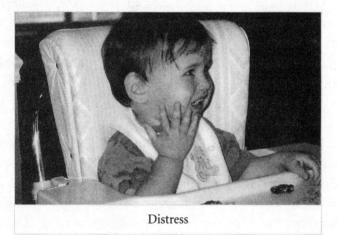

Distress

Ten Possible Triggers of Distress:

- Hunger
- Sustained, loud noises
- Bad smells or tastes
- Loss of a desired object
- Gas
- Pain
- Separation from a person
- Too bright a light or sunshine
- Fatigue
- Dirty diapers

How to Handle Distress

First, Try to Allow Its Expression.
When you let a child communicate distress, you are showing your child that it is okay to experience a full range of emotions. You're telling your child that what she feels is valid. These messages are essential to your child's emerging sense of self and self-confidence. Of course, there may be times—especially in public—when the expression of distress presents difficulties. But these moments can be handled by recognizing the distress signal, validating and labeling it with words, fixing the cause of the distress and, if necessary, taking the infant to another location.

If it is hard for you to hear your child express distress—if you hear yourself saying, "That doesn't really hurt," or "Big boys don't cry," or "Stop making such a fuss"—here are some insights that might make it easier for you to feel comfortable with the expression of distress. Remember, the handling of negative feelings is especially important to the development of tension regulation.

Even the Youngest Infants Feel What They Feel for a Reason. Don't try to squash the feeling of distress by denying its validity. For example, experts in child development suggest that you avoid saying "You're not really upset" or "You don't really want to play with that saucer." The child *is* upset. She is having fun with the saucer. When you tell her that her feelings aren't real, you are making it hard for her to get a good sense of herself or her place in the world. Your role is to provide validation for the child's feeling: "What is it that you're upset about? Can we figure that out and do something about it?" Or, "Isn't that saucer pretty. Let's put it up here so we can all look at it. Or put it on the rug where we can play with it carefully so it won't break."

What Is Often Called "Whining and Complaining" Is Usually the Expression of Distress. We as parents often use critical terms (whining and complaining) to push away the discomfort that we feel when our children are distressed. True, the degree of a young child's upset can sometimes seem out of proportion to what's actually happened. You know your daughter fell down, but it was a minor spill. However, from the child's perspective that spill could represent so much more—surprise, humiliation, confusion, and an intense feeling of vulnerability. If you ignore this reality, focusing only on what you hope is true (your child is just fine), you may engage in interactions that inadvertently bring shame or increased unhappiness and distress to your child.

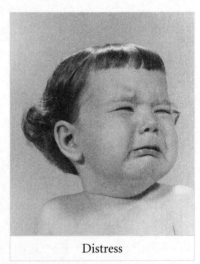

Distress

Virginia Demos framed the problem in terms of sequences of affective expression and response. Say an infant and caregiver are playing happily together. When the play is interrupted, perhaps because the toy is lost or it is time to go home, the child bursts into tears. At this point, the caregiver might respond with something like: "That's okay, we can use these toys instead" or "We'll be back here soon to play again." Her response would most likely decrease the distress and heal the ruptures, with the regaining of positive affect. This type of pattern is positive-negative-positive. However, the caregiver might respond critically and punitively to the infant's negative affect: "Oh, stop your crying!" or "Will you be quiet? That noise is really obnoxious!" In this case, the infant would be left not only with the original hurt but a second one as well. This would create a positive-negative-negative sequence. Demos suggested this sequence is dangerous because the negative affects start a vicious cycle, with no repair of the ruptures, and the result is chronic rage and despair.

I'll never forget once several years ago when I was with my son at the grocery store and a small child walking with his mom took a tumble and started to cry loudly. The mom was so embarrassed by his outburst that she couldn't address his upset but instead began to lecture the child on how it was just a little spill, he wasn't hurt, and big boys don't cry anyway. The child looked up at his mom with such a bewildered expression, reached out his arms hoping for some consolation, and wailed even louder. The mom's discomfort increased as her child's wailing went up in volume until she simply picked up the child, abandoned her grocery cart, and left the store. I turned to my son and said, "What was wrong with that picture?" And he replied with the simple clarity that at times a five-year-old can possess and

Look at Your Motives When You Respond to Distress

Parents often minimize their child's pain to make themselves feel better. If you insist the child "isn't really hurt," or "there's no reason to be so upset," you really may be trying to convince yourself that your child is not in any pain. Sometimes watching your child feel bad is just too uncomfortable, it hurts you too much. But what does insisting that the distress isn't real teach your child? It says: "Feel what I want you to feel and forget about how you *do* feel." It also says: "I can't share your distress and pain. It is too much for me. I'll pretend it doesn't exist." For a child, that is the beginning of difficulty with tension regulation and emotional turmoil, and a short path to low self-esteem.

said, "She didn't get it, did she? She sure is making a lot of trouble for herself today!"

Second, Try to Acknowledge the Child's Feelings.

For example, if your child takes a tumble and is crying, you might react and say: "Oh my, you took a tumble. That didn't feel good, did it? Let's make it feel better." As a result of your acknowledgment of what happened and how it made the child feel, the child is allowed to cry, which is his true emotion, and he is offered reassurance that his emotional response is valid. He is soothed by your empathy with his distress. (Teaching children empathy is a big and important job. They learn much through example.) Try putting into words what happened and what the feelings are. Acknowledging the feelings also helps the child learn tension regulation: After you validate your child's feelings, it is much easier for him to move past his distress and regain composure. Over time, he will make this kind of interaction a part of his own internal world, moving toward self-soothing and tension regulation.

Third, Try to Eliminate the Cause of the Distress.

There are endless potential causes of distress—hunger, fatigue, loud noises, discomfort, or pain, to name a few. As an infant grows and begins to crawl and walk, two of the most common ones are boredom and separation.

Boredom comes from a lack of interesting and enjoyable stimulation. It makes a child feel restless, trapped, unhappy. Some infants and young children can keep themselves interested and intrigued, but most are not self-stimulating until they get older. So, parents who like to help their infants learn—and like to keep the peace—realize early on that it's best to provide a steady stream of calm but engaging stimulation, particularly interaction with other people.

Research by Rene Spitz in the 1950s revealed that infants will actually die if they do not get enough stimulation, even if they have enough food, sustaining shelter, and are clean. His work and work by others over the past five decades has confirmed that if there is not enough appropriate stimulation at certain points in an infant's life, the brain will not develop fully. Intelligence, language skills, perception, thought, and other abilities may be diminished. However, an infant does not have to experience extreme boredom to be affected negatively by lack of stimulation.

Even in ordinary situations, boredom may make infants withdraw and become disengaged or it may lead to chronic fussiness. In young children, it can trigger restlessness and the tendency to get into everything, as they desperately try to stir up some interesting stimulation. Later on, as they enter adolescence, boredom may result in self-destructive, delinquent, or criminal behavior.

I spend a good amount of time reading and writing in local fast food restaurants. That's given me a lot of opportunity to observe what happens when kids get bored. Sometimes, they provide themselves with stimulation by blowing milk through a straw, dropping a fork on the floor, or by giving a glass-shattering yell. Other times they become fussy and squirmy, crying and hitting anyone who tries to restrain them. I remember one day watching a cute toddler sitting with four adults. After her repeated squeals for attention had been completely ignored, she shredded her pancakes, dumped syrup on herself and spilled a cup of coffee—all in a matter of minutes. The adults were horrified and taken completely by surprise. "Why would you do that?" one demanded. Well, if the child could talk, she would have said, "Because you were so rude. When I spoke up and asked for your attention, you completely ignored me! What was I supposed to do?" But since she couldn't, she was soundly smacked on the arm and hauled off to the bathroom for a thorough washing off and, I imagine, scolding.

Over and over I've observed that when boredom/distress reaches such levels, many parents misinterpret the child's outcry as naughty behavior. The parents' impulse is to punish the distress instead of providing the child with something that stimulates interest. Then, the conflict and unhappiness escalate, sometimes leading to yelling and hitting by both parent and child—which has negative consequences for the child's emotional development and the relationship between the two. Even mild-mannered parents, who don't understand the signals, may misinterpret fussiness. They may dismiss it as, "Oh, she just can't stand it when she isn't the center of attention." Or they demean the child by saying, "You are so bad! Why can't you learn to behave?" These responses also dismiss the child's legitimate expression of feelings and can undermine self-esteem.

If your child is acting up in public, chances are she is not being a brat, but is simply asking for something to occupy her curiosity. That may mean that you have to turn your attention away from adult conversation or your own meal and focus on her, but usually providing something of interest will help the situation.

So, if you and your child have to sit for a long time in the doctor's waiting room, try playing with toys, reading a book, walking around the room to look at what's on the wall. At a restaurant, provide favorite toys in the stroller; include your child in the conversation; hold the child if necessary. When shopping, try to include your child in the activities. Attending to a baby's boredom will help provide proper stimulation so that intelligence, language, thought, and perception can develop normally. In fact, these times can be transformed from periods of potential upset into opportunities for learning. "Let's see, this pasta is

$1.09 a box. So, if we get two boxes, then the total is——." "Oh, look at that sign: 'Weigh on this scale.' Weigh, what a great word. It means to find out how heavy something is . . . even you!"

Separation anxiety, another common trigger for distress, is an inevitable part of life—particularly an infant's—and it's difficult to prevent it from happening. Sooner or later, mom and dad have to leave the room, go to work, run an errand, or take a shower. A child may also have to deal with more significant separations, caused by a parent having to travel or by divorce. But whether the separation is part of everyday activities or extraordinary circumstances, infants can quickly conclude that they are being abandoned, and this may make them feel vulnerable and unprotected. In such circumstances, your emphasis can be on acknowledging the child's feelings. For example, if your child becomes upset when your wife leaves the house to run errands, you might say, "I think you must be missing Mommy. I love you, sweetie, and Mommy will be back soon. For now, here's Teddy. Maybe if you hugged him close, you'd feel better. Or would you like to bundle up in Mommy's old sweater? And here's a picture of Mommy and you!" Even if the infant cannot talk yet, she understands the tone of voice and general meaning.

In these moments of separation/distress a child may also turn angry—at you who are there and at the person who has left them. It is important not to take this anger personally. The child is simply expressing escalated, sustained distress and is pleading to be soothed and reassured. If you think there is nothing you can do, think again.

Attachment and separation issues are quite complex, and they have been the focus of much research. Infants and children tend to go back and forth between their striving for autonomy and their longing for closeness and security. They are striving to become independent, but they desperately need the reassurance and protection that comes from being very close to mom and dad. A once sociable child may become clingy and timid; a child who loved her babysitter may now act as if they never met; loved grandparents may become resented substitutes for mom or dad. Their interests swing between novelty and the familiar. Some children may have a harder transition to independence than others, but there is no reason to criticize a child who is struggling with this developmental stage. *Remember to talk, explain, substitute, and distract: This is the mantra for handling separation distress.*

Frank is the father of fifteen-month-old John. When his wife had to leave town for four days, the baby was understandably upset and confused. "I did what I could to reassure him," Frank recalls. "I remember when I was changing his diapers, he looked so bewildered. I said, 'I know this must seem different to you, but we can have fun, too. Mom will be back in a few days. Don't worry. I'll take care of everything.' Maybe it was my imagination, but I swear he smiled at me and I could feel his whole body relax. We also sat and cuddled with Mommy's bathrobe, which is very soft, smells like Mom, and John loves it. It made him feel connected to her, I think." This kind of transitional object can be very comforting to kids. Frank did a good job.

It is also helpful if mom or dad can call during their absence and say hello over the phone. A lot of adults think that with kids, out of sight is out of mind. But even if a child is quiet and seemingly adjusting well to the separation, there's a good chance that inside there is some degree of turmoil and emotional upset. Often parents think they will only upset their child if they get in touch with them during their absence. "She's okay, why upset her?" But the parents may be not realize that the child's lack of overt expression of distress may mask her inner emotional state. If the child becomes teary when you call, it is not that you are creating a new feeling of unhappiness, you are simply tapping into the child's unexpressed distress that was there all along. Allowing her to express it and then offering consolation is actually healthy for the child, even if it is traumatic for mom or dad.

Separation distress can also arise over lost objects, with further misunderstandings frequently contributing to the problem. My son and I were recently on the train. Sitting near us was a family with a five-year old who had apparently lost her new fifty-cent, glowing carnival bracelet on the cab ride to the train. She was continuing to be upset over it. The mom was unsympathetic and a bit angry. She kept saying, "I told you that it would get lost if you took it off and played with it in the cab. It's your fault. Now maybe you will listen to me when I warn you about things like that." The little girl looked even more distraught, her lower lip quivering as she tried not to cry. My son whispered to me, "That mom doesn't seem to understand what's going on, does she?" I turned to him and asked, "Should we chat with them a bit?" He agreed, and after a little discussion with the family about what had happened, I said something like, "Your little girl is distressed about losing her bracelet. What a shame. And it really can be annoying for parents to have kids not keep track of something, lose it, and then get all bent out of shape. But it seems like she feels lousy enough already. Maybe just telling her you are sorry she lost it would work better than criticism." The mom seemed to regroup a bit, and said to the child: "I *am* sorry you lost your bracelet." The child dissolved into tears. "She doesn't usually get upset like this," her mom said, startled by the outburst. I explained that the crying was okay. It was a natural expression of bottled-up feelings of distress and relief at being understood. We continued to talk, the kids began playing together, and we all ended up having a really great time on the train ride.

Now, a lot is happening in this example, some of it quite

complicated. But the main point is that an effort was made to allow the expression of distress, and that the distress and anger in both the child and the mother were recognized, acknowledged, and validated, with a very positive result.

The Benefits of Attending to Distress

In the short term, easing your child's distress avoids all kinds of hassles—for you and for baby. A fussy, inconsolable child is tough to handle. It frays your nerves. And it can make you feel incompetent or guilty. Dodge those bullets and you and your child will have a lot more fun together.

In the long term, responding appropriately to distress has many profound benefits for your child. It helps develop tension regulation: Soothing your child now puts her on the road to self-soothing later. It also increases your baby's sense of optimism and buoyancy. Your appropriate response to distress offers reassurance that the world is an okay place. Baby feels, "I'm safe; it's not that scary. My needs will be recognized and attended to." This contributes to baby's emerging sense of competency. You are telling him that his feelings are real and reasonable and that he's judged the events accurately. Your child learns to trust his perceptions of his internal and external world and to express emotions honestly. All this results in a solid sense of self-esteem. By tending to a child's boredom or loss or pain, you are saying, "How you feel is important to me, and you are worth the effort it takes to understand and help you feel better."

Anger

All the negative affects [signals] trouble human beings deeply. . . . Anger is problematic above all.

—Silvan Tomkins, *Affect Imagery Consciousness, Vol. III*

Anger is signaled by a clenched jaw, lips compressed or drawn back to expose teeth, a red face, a frown, eyes may be narrowed, nostrils distended, neck muscles strained, crying, screaming, hitting, kicking, or biting. It is also signaled by sullen withdrawal and glaring. It exists on a continuum from anger to rage.

I remember the first time I realized that Charlie was capable of becoming angry—I mean really mad. He must have been about five months old and he got his foot all tangled up in his blanket and the crib bars while he was taking a nap. I heard him fussing and figured it was nothing, it would pass and he'd go back to sleep. But his fussing continued, and eventually he was wailing. By the time I got into his room, he was furious. His little face was bright red, he was frowning and his mouth was set in the most ferocious expression. You could just tell he wanted to pound something! I felt so bad. But I had no idea that he was in real distress when he started fussing. That taught me that even babies can get mad if they aren't given help when they need it.

—Suzanne, twenty-six, mother of
Charlie, now thirteen months

ANGER MAY BE THE SIGNAL THAT IS TOUGHEST ON PARENTS AND most often misunderstood. It's so hard not to take it personally; and an angry child can be hard to console. So let's take a step back and look at what anger is, how it arises, and what it means.

First of all, it is important to remember that anger is a signal that is hardwired into the brain. When infants and young children get angry, they cannot help it. Kids start out without much ability to control anger; gradually, through your example and your response, they learn how to manage it. An important part of growing up is understanding anger and how to express it appropriately. But this takes time. As they are learning, you may be challenged by the intensity of your young one's emotion.

Anger results when a negative signal, such as distress, is sustained and becomes excessive. An angry baby is saying, "My distress has become too intense for me to bear." Whenever anger arises, the question to ask yourself is, "What triggered the initial distress?" Then you can try to act promptly to remedy the situation. Respond to the cause, try not to react to the content of the anger itself.

It may be easier to see how distress leads to anger if you think about what happens when you stub your toe. At first, when you hit your toe hard against the bed post, you feel pain and distress . . . but seconds later, as the increased pain becomes more apparent, you start feeling angry! All you want to

Anger: "The roar of rage"

do is to swear or hit something. Interestingly, a distressed infant or child has a similar reaction. Perhaps you noticed it when your child tripped and fell into a coffee table. Initially, she may have let out a howl and cried, but then she got mad at you or the table.

Furthermore, anger is not just triggered by an excess of negative signals such as fear, it can also be triggered when the positive signals of interest and enjoyment are interrupted. This leads to distress, which can then turn to anger.

Once you learn to recognize when your child is experiencing excessive distress and then getting angry, the key is to ease the upset. Don't argue with the child or try to squelch the anger; instead focus on what triggers it. It is also important to recognize and control your own anger that may arise in reaction to your child's outburst.

If you can follow these steps, your baby will begin to connect your process of acknowledging the anger, helping to remove the trigger, and controlling your own reaction with positive change. This is how a child learns that spiraling out of control and meltdowns aren't necessary. You may not be able to do this from the start, but over time, if you follow these basic steps, you may learn to handle your child's various expressions of anger. And so will your child.

I have a colleague, Pam, who told me this story about a mom named Nancy and her year-and-a-half-old son Jerry, who was having ever more intense temper tantrums. My colleague first met Nancy and Jerry in a small preschool class for newborns to three-year-olds. Jerry was playing happily with an adult-size snow shovel when a younger child toddled too close to the blade of the shovel. At that point, one of the teachers came over and gently but firmly took the shovel away from Jerry and hid it behind a curtain. "It's just too dangerous," she told the child. Well, Jerry went ballistic. He screamed, cried, lay down on his back, kicked his feet and bumped his head on the floor. And it didn't stop. Nancy came over, shook her head in embarrassment, and said, "I just leave him alone when he gets like this. He gets over it." And then under her breath she muttered, "He always does this. It makes me so mad!"

After a while Jerry did quiet down and my colleague noticed that he was pale, lethargic, and drained looking. Pam knew that both Nancy and her son, Jerry, were bright and quick, so what was going awry, she wondered?

Nancy came up to Pam the next week and said: "I'm sure you saw what happened last week. I'm trying to be a good mom, but I wish I knew what the heck was going on." Pam asked her for some more details about how Jerry was behaving. As Nancy talked, two major themes emerged. First, Jerry had begun having temper tantrums at quite a young age and they had become more frequent and more intense. And second, Nancy really hated anger and didn't like to be around it. She believed anger should be curbed as quickly and efficiently as possible. "No good ever comes from getting angry," she said. Clearly, Nancy was horrified to see that her worst nightmare—an angry child—was becoming her reality.

Nancy, like most parents, loved her child and genuinely wanted to do a good job of raising him. So, Pam decided the best place to start was by giving her some basic information about infancy and the nine inborn signals. In particular, Pam felt that it might help to convey what anger actually was—a hardwired instinctive response to interrupted interest and excessive distress. She also felt that it might be useful to explore the feelings of low self-esteem that Nancy was experiencing as a result of her problems with Jerry.

Pam told Nancy about how researchers had discovered that anger was one of the inborn, natural responses that all babies have. They discussed the signal for interest, and how babies are stimulus-seeking and curious, and how interrupting their expressions of interest invariably results in anger. That is exactly what had happened in the incident with the snow shovel. Jerry's interest had been unceremoniously interrupted and no one attempted to explain sufficiently to him what was happening or to offer an alternative source of stimulation and interest. Pam explained to Nancy how important it was to talk to Jerry about why the shovel was being taken away, about how it made him feel, and what could be done to provide a substitute. Even if he didn't understand all the words, he would understand that the adults in his life were tuned in to his emotional needs and were helping him learn how to regulate his anger and redirect his attention. Pam suggested Nancy try saying things such as: "Honey, I'm sorry but we have to move the shovel, the blade is too sharp and someone might get hurt. I know it's upsetting but we have to put it over here. It's okay to be angry with me. I know you were having fun. But let's look at this helicopter over here. No? Not any fun? What would you like to play with instead?" Or, "Let's look at the shovel together and take a look at that sharp blade."

Nancy and Jerry's relationship didn't improve immediately, but over several weeks, they began to communicate better. "It makes so much sense, this anger thing," Nancy told Pam. "I just think of anger as a signal now and look for the cause and try to do something about that. I don't take it so personally, and it doesn't scare me so much."

Nancy also began to talk more about how she had felt like such a failure as a mom. Once Jerry had started getting angry, she became less and less sure of her abilities as a mom and less able to recognize what her son was trying to communicate. Now, as she learned to deal with his anger more appropriately and constructively, Jerry's tantrums began to subside and Nancy began to gain confidence. About six months later, Pam and Nancy had a chance to meet again. Nancy said things continued to go well and she had been reading a lot about anger and other feelings. The reading had helped her not only with Jerry but with her own inner life as well.

As an adult, being able to recognize anger and deal appropriately with the triggers is essential. With a child, recognizing and verbally labeling the anger are important. This way you can take care of what set it off. This means you shouldn't try to sweep it under the rug when it comes up. Anger denied gets bottled up inside. Even in small children, the anger can then be transformed into depression, sullenness, pessimism, or chronic rage toward oneself or others.

The Timeline: What Triggers Anger?

- Babies usually express distress because of hunger, fatigue, pain, and sometimes illness. Older infants may feel distress for an ever expanding number of reasons—various frustrations or boredom, for example.

- As the infant gets older and increasingly more verbal, the triggers of distress are likely to become ever more complex and psychological (associated with feelings of disappointment, shame, humiliation, fear, loneliness, a sense of abandonment, tension).

- At any age, anger can arise if any signal becomes too intense, or shifts into distress that is excessive and sustained. Interruption of interest also can produce anger—that's why your child may become particularly upset when you have to call a halt to what he feels is a great time.

How to Attend to Anger

Coping with your child's anger requires you to handle your own emotional responses first. Technically, anger is considered to be a highly contagious affect—that is, anger in one person readily leads to anger in the person with whom he is dealing. Thus, for many parents a child's anger may be contagious—they become angry in response. Often, parents don't recognize anger as an inherent, natural response to specific stimuli or a cry of distress. Instead, they see it as a personal attack and react defensively. However, if you control your own anger when confronted by your child's, your child will begin to connect this process of acknowledging the anger, helping to remove the trigger, and controlling your own reaction to the anger with positive change. This is how a child learns that spiraling out of control and meltdowns aren't necessary. This is the road to self-soothing and tension regulation.

This is not always easy to do, however. I once knew of a mother who would become so angry at her children when they expressed anger that she would say, "Okay, I've had it." She would pack their bags with clothing and put the kids in the car, "to take them to the orphanage." The kids would then break down and apologize and cry and tell their mom she was the best mom in the world and they weren't angry at her. Having won, she'd take them home, feeling they had learned a lesson. But it was not the lesson she intended. What they did learn was that if they expressed any anger, it threatened to completely destroy their mother and her love for them. The potential damage to their emotional development was profound. Another mother I was acquainted with would lock her children on the porch when they got mad at her and tell them that a fictitious Mrs. Smith was coming to take them away.

These kinds of extreme reactions to a child's anger often arise when the parent has a low sense of self-worth and a poor understanding of feelings. The child's anger confirms the parent's feelings that she is a terrible person. As a result, the parent may strike out to remove the cause of her own distressful emotions. Parents who have such reactions to their children's anger might find it helpful to remember that when they hear anger, they should think *distress,* not *attack.*

Some parents have a different type of reaction to anger. They are afraid of it, so they try to bottle it up and make it disappear without really dealing with the signal and its meaning. And other parents may be afraid of expressing their own, not well controlled, anger. If that sounds familiar to you, you might try calling a time out for yourself. Again, it is always best to put water on the fire, not gasoline. But before you walk away, take the time to put your emotions into words and to explain to your child what is going on. Tell your child, "Look, I'm just too angry to deal with this. But it doesn't mean I don't love you. I am angry at this behavior and I don't know if I can control my anger. I might say something or do something I'll regret. I need a time out."

Ask yourself, how do I handle anger? What do I think and feel about it? If you sense you are uncomfortable with or unable to control anger in yourself, try to analyze where your feelings come from and get a handle on them. Ask: How did my family deal with anger? How do I express anger in adult relationships, today? You may see that there are some interesting correlations between your personal reactions to anger and your child's angry outbursts. This may help you gain control of your reactions and modify your response to your child's signal for anger.

You may well feel anger in response to your child's outbursts—but you hopefully have a better ability than your child does to regulate your emotions and to know what behaviors are appropriate. When your child signals anger you have the opportunity to act as a role model for the wise handling of emotions: If the child sees you manage your anger well, she will learn how to do the same. As we discussed in Chapter 7, on identification, you are your child's prime source of information about reactions to life's many complex situations and about how to express emotions. If you get into a screaming rage in traffic jams, your child will learn that this kind of expression of anger is an appropriate response to frustration. If you yell when you are tired, grumpy, hungry, or displeased, your child will think this is the way he should behave in such situations as well. But if you understand how these emotions work, validate your own feelings, develop a playful attitude about frustrations, and are resourceful about finding ways to cope with difficulties, then your child will learn to be more easygoing as well.

So next time your child blows a fuse, you can look on it as a golden opportunity to teach self-regulation. Remembering that anger comes from excessive distress, your effort to ease his discomfort acknowledges his pain or frustration, and validates the child's perception of his world. Most importantly, you are showing him *how to problem solve and self-regulate* by your calm coping with the situation. Ultimately, the baby can internalize this *capacity to observe and regulate* and have a sense of *confidence* that if things go wrong and distress or anger sets in, that somehow someone, somewhere (and later himself) can figure out what the problem is and do something about it.

The next thing to do is to put the feelings—yours and his—into words. This will help you regulate your own tension and provide a good role model for your child's developing capacity to regulate his own tension. Talk to your child about the angry outburst. If he threw his peanut butter sandwich across the floor, ask what was distressing: Not hungry? Not feeling good? Wrong kind of peanut butter? Expecting something else? Then perhaps you can more beneficially explore the behavior of throwing the sandwich. And finally, go through a mental checklist when the signal for anger appears: Ask yourself, Is my child hungry? Tired? In need of a clean diaper? In pain or physical discomfort? If the answers to those questions are no, think about the possibility that your child is getting sick or teething. Ideally, you will learn not to take your child's anger personally and you will not get as angry yourself.

You may also work to reduce the intensity of your child's anger by acknowledging the anger—don't stifle it or deny or criticize it or ridicule it—and then focusing entirely on taking care of the situation that triggered it. For example: You've put your child into his high chair and given him a car to play with. He's eating and playing with the car at the same time. When the car falls, the baby starts whimpering. You ignore it, figuring he should be concentrating on his food anyway. He continues to whimper. "Eat your sweet potatoes," you suggest nicely. Suddenly, the kid explodes, crying and banging on his tray because you won't pick up the car for him. You become impatient and snap, "Come on. Start eating. Enough with the car." Now your baby is in a rage. His face turns red, his fists are clenched, and he starts to scream. Finally, you see the importance of the car, pick it up, and gently say "Okay. Here's the car." If your tone is not critical, but rather soft and soothing, there's a good chance the baby will stop crying. He has "spoken," and he has been heard.

If on the other hand, you refuse to return the car, the situation can degenerate into a battle of wills. It's you versus your child: you, insisting that you are the three-hundred-pound gorilla who gets to do whatever he likes (and remember, from a child's point of view that is exactly what you are anyway), and your child, who's fighting as hard as he can to be understood and to get you to help him remedy a situation (the dropped car) he is powerless to fix (he cannot get out of the chair and retrieve the car).

The final point to remember is that there are always alternatives—if you have to interrupt your child's expression of interest, there are many other activities or objects available that can re-stimulate interest. The trick is to think of them instead of simply reacting.

Sometimes, however, all the best management skills at your command won't work. Anger may have its own momentum. It may be the result of an accumulation of frustrations, a reaction to "the last straw." There may be no one trigger for the distress and no simple way to offer solace to your child. Or, anger may simply feed on itself. Your child may be so revved up that it becomes difficult for him to calm down. When that happens, it may take some time to restore equilibrium. If your child is biting or throwing things, you may need to do whatever you can do to cool down the situation. You can sort out what happened later. You may have to contain your child by holding him in your lap, or you may say, "I'm just going to leave you alone. Here are your stuffed animals." After your child has calmed down you can talk to him about what happened.

Fear

[Fear] is a response that is very toxic even in small doses. [Fear] is an overly compelling persuader designed for emergency motivation of a life-and-death significance. In all animals such a response has the essential biological function of guaranteeing that the preservation of the life of the organism has a priority second to none.

—Silvan Tomkins, *Affect Imagery Consciousness, Vol. III*

The signal for fear is expressed in several ways. A baby's eyes may be frozen open, her skin pale. She may become cold or start sweating. Her face, hands, and legs may tremble. Her hair may even stand up on end, and she may be very still or cry out. Young infants often react by

187

withdrawing completely or suddenly falling asleep. Fear is on a continuum from fear to terror.

When my son was about eight months old, we took him to his first fireworks display after a baseball game. We were very excited about it, figuring that he would love the colors. But with the first explosion he was startled, and he was terrorized by the second. Shortly thereafter he grabbed on to his mother, burying his head in her arms. The loud noise was simply too much for him to take in. Although we tried to convince him that it was safe and beautiful to look at, there was no easing his discomfort. We left, quickly, to spare him further distress. As the booming continued, his face became kind of frozen, he sort of zoned out, went into himself, and fell asleep. I think it was to protect himself. Even after we got to the car and drove, and things were quiet, he stayed asleep for some time. In this situation, we had made a big effort to have this family outing, and it was initially difficult to give his feelings the respect they deserved. But the only solution was to say, "Oh, that's a loud noise. Here, let me cover your ears for you. Don't worry. We'll make it go away." And then head for the car and get out of there. When you are a parent, the child's needs come first, and when he needs to have his fear eased it is particularly important to recognize that the feeling is valid and must be addressed. Just a few years later, after some exposure to fireworks on television, we talked with him about fireworks and about his first fireworks encounter, and then took him to another display. He absolutely loved it and has enjoyed fireworks ever since.

—Paul C. Holinger

FEAR IS A NATURAL AND NECESSARY REACTION—IT HELPS A PERSON avoid danger by sending an alarm throughout the body, pumping up stress hormones, preparing the mind and body for dealing with possible peril. No one, not even a baby, could survive without the capacity to feel and react to fear. Fear is an alarm bell and children ring it loud and clear, perhaps because they cannot protect themselves and they need to alert you to come to their assistance.

In the brain, fear is associated with a relatively sudden onset and steep increase in the rate of neural firing, more sudden and steeper than interest but with less rapid increase than surprise. Fear is quite toxic; the body and brain cannot tolerate the biochemical

reactions for long. However, single events that cause fear usually do not harm a child in the long term. It is frequent and unresolved triggers of fear that can cause problems. That's why it's important to try to intervene effectively and resolve the situation.

When you are sensitive to the signal for fear and help resolve the situation, your child learns about fear and about regulating it—it is

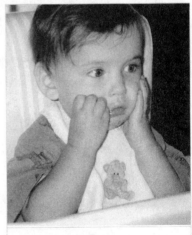

Fear

part of his emerging mastery of his outer environment and inner psychological world.

It is important, however, to realize that what may scare one child may simply startle or provoke interest in another. Some children are more reactive and sensitive to certain sensory inputs than others, making them more easily startled or fearful. Because the world is such a strange new place, many different events can trigger the signal for fear in a child—an overwhelming sensation (a first ride on a swing or an encounter with a strange dog), a loud, sudden noise or bright light, for example. These are every-day events that can surprise and alarm a child. Halloween masks, or clowns, often scare very young children. This is apparently due to the distortion of the face, which, of course, is the main area for sending the emotional signals.

A child may develop an ongoing fear from a seemingly triv-ial set of episodes. A big dog comes loping up; your child becomes scared and looks to you for resolution. But you don't notice the signals she is putting out, or you know for a fact that the dog is no threat to your child. Either way you fail to realize your child isn't on your wavelength. "Hey, this is a nice dog, say hello," you suggest. The child is horrified that you'd thrust her toward the gaping maw of the ferocious beast. (Imagine you are smaller than a golden retriever.) Pretty soon, fear hits and you've got a terrified kid on your hands. After a couple more run-ins with dogs that scare the child—coupled with your lack of sensitivity to the child's signal—you may have a child who feels increasingly vulnerable and unprotected with dogs, but perhaps also in general. Such fears may become a part of your child's personality if they are frequent and there is no escape or resolution.

Another reason that children may express fear is because

they also are struggling with their own anger or distress. If they have poor regulation of those feelings, they may project their anger onto the outside world, attributing menace and peril to a wide variety of events. This can lead to fear-stricken behavior and troubling nightmares for toddlers and young children. I remember one young child who told me about a dream in which her stuffed animals came to life and her favorite one was cut in half. She was terrorized by this and was weepy and anxious for days afterwards. The resolution of the problem was complex, but in part it required that the parents become aware of and change their tendency to be uncomfortable with any expressions of anger. Their usual response, whenever their daughter became angry, was to reprimand her sternly and tell her that nice girls don't behave like that. But once they were able to understand what they were doing and see how it affected their child, they could begin to allow her to express anger. As a result, the child was able to begin being more comfortable with her own angry feelings, and the intense scary nightmares dissipated.

Fearfulness, whether during sleep or during the day, is well worth paying attention to. It may be related to scary external events, or to internal difficulties in managing various feelings and tensions. Distress and anger are often associated with fear.

Sometimes, fear becomes damaging as a result of profoundly traumatic or recurring negative experiences. For everyone, adult or child, chronic or traumatic fear poisons the body and the mind. In a small child the potential damage is great. If a child encounters repeated abuse or violence or witnesses it between his parents, for example, his fear response can get stuck in overdrive. This in turn can increase the risk of behavioral and emotional disorders sooner or later.

Attending to Fear

Fear is a difficult signal to manage appropriately: It's necessary and healthy, yet it's potentially toxic. You, as a parent, may hate to see it expressed. When baby is fearful, you may simply swoop down and try to deny the signal as quickly as possible, saying, "Oh, that's not scary." But, as with all signals, fear needs its due. Again, it may help you to remember the basics: Allow the expression of fear, label the feeling, and do something about the trigger. Granting that your child has a right to be afraid begins to give him the tools to handle fear and starts the process of accurately sorting out his perceptions about his inner and outer world. The easiest way to do this is to label the fear for the child. If you get in a crowded elevator and your child seems scared, say "This elevator is a bit scary, huh? Too many strangers? Too bumpy? We'll be out of it soon." But don't impose your fears on the child. If elevators scare you—a touch of claustrophobia, perhaps—don't plant the idea in the child's mind by sharing your particular anxiety. Your goal is to respond to the child's signal of fear, not to activate it.

In day-to-day situations, when your child may express fear, you want to validate the feeling by acknowledging it and labeling it for your child. Don't try to suppress it or shut it off. It may seem strange that your little one is afraid of bald men or people wearing sunglasses, but it's not. Offer reassurance, explanation and, when possible, remove the baby from the frightening situation. A child cannot control her reactions; she doesn't choose to be afraid; it is not a reflection of a weak character.

In addition to removing the trigger of fear (for example, the scary dog), another strategy is to help your child transform fear into interest. In the case of the dog, you might respond by picking up your child and saying, "I know this dog looks scary and big, but now I've picked you up and he can't get you. Now we can look at him. Isn't his coat a pretty color of brown? See how his tail wags."

A comforting transitional object such as a teddy bear or blanket that the child can use for self-soothing may be particularly helpful. There's no need to discourage the use of such objects. Children will use them as long as they need them and put them aside according to their own timetable.

It is also important to avoid using shame to counteract your child's fears. For example, you may provoke feelings of shame if you say things such as: "What's with you? You're being silly. There is absolutely nothing to be afraid of. You're such a wimp." This will only teach the child to deny fear and become macho or bullying about fearful emotions. The "buck up" school of child rearing doesn't actually make for strong children. Over the years I've collected a list of callous responses that parents sometimes say to scared children, often with the best of intentions: Enough is enough; simmer down; shut up; stop crying or I will really give you something to cry about; don't tell me your troubles, I've got enough of my own. These kinds of statements undermine the child's confidence in his own perceptions of the world, and make him feel that there is no protection or security available. Telling a young child that she is "wrong" or "bad" or "dumb" or "acting like a baby" or using any other kind of shaming criticism can only make her feel confused about how she feels and suspect she is wrong to feel it in the first place. It completely undercuts her emerging sense of identity and self-esteem. Just as with the opening story about taking my son to the fireworks display, it's best not to debate a child's response, but to understand it, label it, and act quickly to ease the fear.

Another important method for minimizing fear is to eliminate it from your bag of parenting techniques. Fear is not a good motivator long-term. ("Eat your peas or you're going to get a spanking.") Fear makes children feel dread and apprehension and it constricts a child's stimulus-seeking nature, thus compromising learning. This can make a child afraid of new people and experiences and turn the world into a sinister-seeming place. Fear can also cause lying. When a child is anxious or fearful of what will happen, he may lie to avoid the dreaded result of telling the truth. Fear is a powerful emotion and you have a great deal of influence over how it shapes your baby's inner life.

One of the toughest situations to handle is when your child does something that is dangerous, such as running out into the street. Many parents feel that using fear to make sure the child never does it again is the only effective solution. They grab the child, perhaps deliver a spanking, and say, "Don't you ever do that again. You could get killed." But even in these kinds of situations, it is more effective to offer a firm but compassionate verbal explanation of the rules of conduct and the danger, instead of hitting. The whole issue of "stranger danger" is another area in which using fear as a way to enforce behavior can backfire. While a child needs to learn to evaluate the world and tune in to situations and people that are not safe, a blanket condemnation of all new situations, people, and encounters is both unrealistic and terrorizing, and it limits a child's ability to explore and learn.

Coping with Situations
of Abuse or Violence

If you or your child are in a situation where you are subjected to violence or abuse or must witness it being inflicted on others, it is crucial to protect the child—and yourself—and remove both of you from the situation. These situations are often quite complicated and this solution may be much easier said than done. But there are alternatives: shelters, friends, relatives, halfway houses, a bus ride out of town. What is important to be clear about is that remaining in a traumatic, violent situation is very detrimental to your child's well-being. Violence and abuse exact a tremendous emotional price.

On the other hand, if you find that *you* are the source of the abuse or violence, if you cannot control your temper, you should seek help immediately and remove your child to a safe place with a safe caretaker until you are able to get control of your impulses and treat your child with love and understanding. This doesn't mean that you never get angry at your child—kids are tremendously draining and provocative. All parents feel anger toward their children at one time or another. But the edge of danger and threat of physically hurting the child must be removed.

Hitting a child is a form of terror. Spanking is a hit with a fancy name. If you find that you spank your child, it means you have run out of alternative ways of dealing with situations and need to expand your repertoire of emotional and physical responses. Spanking backfires as a motivator of good behavior. You may gain your child's superficial compliance with your wishes, but his inner world will be filled with anxiety and rage. One parent I met routinely used his belt to discipline his young child; as a result the child became almost mute, fearing expression of any emotion for fear of getting hit. The results were devastating to the child's emerging sense of self. In addition, the volcanic, unexpressed anger the child felt did not bode well for his adult psyche or relationships. Only when the father was slowly helped to see that he was increasing the potential for serious conflict with his son, and was helped to increase his own competency as a parent, were he and his son able to begin to repair their relationship and their own damaged inner selves.

The Benefits of Addressing Fear

When you help your child manage her fears and remove fear from your bag of parenting tricks, your child can become a brave explorer of ideas and places and people. Children without inappropriate fear are much more optimistic and buoyant; they feel pleasure more deeply and are less ashamed of their inner feelings. In addition, validating and managing your child's fears teaches her how to be wisely self-protective and emotionally honest.

Shame

Shame is the affect of indignity, of defeat, of transgression and of alienation.

> —Silvan Tomkins, *Affect Imagery Consciousness, Vol. III*

A baby signals shame with downcast eyes and slumping shoulders; his face and neck muscles sag downward. He may avert his head or look down; eyelids droop. Some babies even blush. The signal may be experienced on a continuum from slight shame to intense humiliation.

Some of my earliest memories are of my parents putting me down, ridiculing me, making me feel that I was terrible.

One of their favorite expressions was, "Well, you don't feel like such a big shot now, do you?" They'd say it whenever I messed up, maybe spilled some food or dropped something. Another was, "God is watching, so you better not do anything wrong. Even if I'm not around, God is and he'll catch you!" I can tell you, at the age of four, I spent a lot of time wondering why they thought what I was doing was wrong. I was sure my parents were ashamed of me. Today, my mom would be shocked to hear that. She never thought she was doing anything that would hurt me, but she comes from the old school and she believes kids should not be "coddled," that was her word for it. She also hoped they would be seen but not heard. Guilt, shame, self-doubt, I've had to fight those feelings all my life. With my own kids, I am vigilant about not putting them down or making them feel bad for doing "kid things." Instead, I try to support and praise them . . . this strategy has done wonders.

—Stephen, thirty-three, father
of two children, two and four

FOR A CHILD, THE WORLD CAN BE ONE HUGE PLAYGROUND MADE for discovery and adventure. For mom and dad, it is often a place where disaster lurks around every corner and their child's expression of interest or enjoyment always seems to be a prelude to a mess—thrown food, spilled milk, torn books, scattered dishes. The combination of exuberance unbound and the understandable parental impulse to create order is a potential formula for shame.

Interest and enjoyment + interference and disapproval = shame

Shame is a complex inborn signal. There is a great deal of debate about its origins and timing of onset, and I am not going to resolve those issues here. What I hope to do is explain how children express shame and how it relates to other signals, thereby helping you avoid the miscommunications that can trigger the harmful aspects of shame.

Technically, shame is one of the nine built-in signals. It is marked by slumped shoulders, downcast eyes, and averted head. Shame is triggered by an interference with or an inhibition of the positive signals of interest and enjoyment. It involves a mismatch between the expectations of the infant and the response of the caregiver. It is as if the infant,

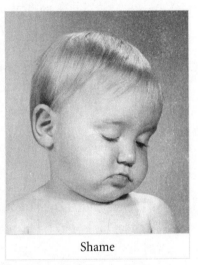

Shame

intentionally pouring out her milk, says: "Oh Mom! Look at how neat that milk looks cascading off the high chair onto the floor . . . and the splashes! How cool!" And Mom replies: "What in the world are you doing? Stop that. Don't ever do that again. Now look at what a mess you've caused, and I have to clean it up!"

Psychologically, shame appears to underlie a sense of inferiority, guilt, shyness, and discouragement. It can dampen interest, fuel distress and, when extreme, it may trigger anger. Feelings of inadequacy or inferiority are often associated with shame. As I mentioned, in children shame is stimulated when their expressions of interest and enjoyment are met with disapproval or mis-understanding on the part of parents or caretakers. Since much of the development of a positive sense of self involves interest and enjoyment, frequent and inappropriate triggering of shame leads to problems with self-esteem.

Common Triggers of Shame

Whenever a child's natural impulses and interests clash with the outside world's constraints, rules, or attitudes, shame may arise. Shame itself is not necessarily bad. As the psychoanalyst Michael Basch commented, feeling mild shame tells a child (or adult) that certain conduct is socially unacceptable. Shame says, "Stop and think about the current situation and what you are doing." However, children may feel excessive shame when parents set limits on behavior. This happens when parents mistakenly voice their objections to a child's behavior by criticizing the child himself and not simply his inappropriate actions. In doing that, parents create in that child the sense that he is somehow wrong at the core, that his impulse to express interest or enjoyment is a character flaw.

The misuse of shame can be harmful. For example, if you shame a child by focusing not on an undesirable behavior but on the child himself, or if you use intense shame to change behavior, you may cause devastating damage to the child's self-esteem. The good news is that in most situations of unacceptable behavior, you can use your child's positive feelings of interest and enjoyment to communicate your wish for a change in behavior: "Oh, now that's interesting. Look at that milk spilled all over the floor. What a pattern it makes. But I have to tell you, I'm not thrilled with your behavior. I love you, but that's no way to learn about milk. Here, let me show you how it works. You take your cup in both hands and bring it up to your mouth so it doesn't spill. That's how you do it. Now let's clean this up. See how the paper towel soaks it up?"

Nonetheless, even if you are exceedingly adept at handling your child's expressions of signals, he may end up feeling shame. It is part of being human. The capacity to feel and express shame is a built-in response to the interruption of interest and enjoyment. Take, for example, a baby's bowel movement. To a kid, once he is aware of what is happening, having a bowel movement is a pretty marvelous act, nothing to feel aversion toward, nothing to be embarrassed about; in fact, it's to be reveled in. Well, the act of changing a dirty diaper, throwing away the excrement, cleaning off the baby's bottom, maybe making a comment on the smell or look of the diaper, can plant the seeds of shame about bodily functions in a child's mind. The very process of civilizing a baby could be seen in part as a process of instilling societal norms for shame. In our society, we wear clothes to cover our bodies. That act, so unnatural to a child, may elicit shame. In cultures where people wear only minimal covering, shame about exposing the body may be minimal.

To avoid triggering shame, the trick is to set limits, teach manners, and instill a sense of right and wrong without stifling interest or enjoyment. It can be done, but it means being vigilant about separating your instructions about what are desirable actions from criticism of the child herself. For example, when your child takes your books off the shelf and tears the pages, you might let her know that books are interesting and offer her one of her own to look at, while moving her away from the bookshelf. Then you can tell her that she shouldn't tear books, they are for reading. And the two of you can sit together and look at her book. She is learning limits, but is not being told that her interest in books is bad.

I know a woman who remembers very distinctly the battles between her mother and herself over food spilled on the floor. "Whenever I dropped food on the floor my mom would say, 'Pick that up now. You don't want to get germs on it!' She made it seem very dangerous to encounter germs, whatever they were. But I would sit and stare at the food, trying to figure out exactly how germs worked. I thought if the food landed on the germs then they would already be on the food and it couldn't get any worse, so what's the rush? But, if the food became more germ-covered the longer it sat on the floor, then that meant distant germs somehow got the message that the food was there and traveled across the floor to get on the food. I wanted to see this process. So I stared at the food, wondering what was going on with those germs. I couldn't express any of this, of course, and so I seemed to be stubbornly turning a deaf ear to my mother and she would become enraged. It made me feel very confused about what was right and wrong. I've never forgotten that, and it has changed how I think about children's experiences of the world. I always try to explain how things work and to tell my children why I ask them to do something. There's a lot going on in those little minds and those thoughts deserve respect, even if they are as invisible as those stupid germs my mother was always talking about."

Another common situation can lead to feelings of shame: A child may spill her food all over the floor and look on delightedly as it forms interesting patterns and swirling colors. You may react negatively and say, "Look what you did, you are such a klutz," or "You are bad, don't do that again!" In this situation, your child is criticized for her interest in the food's changing shape and for her basic nature, all at the same time. What you may fail to appreciate is that the whole process of spilling food is wonderful for your child. She loves the noise, the shape of the fallen food or liquid, the droplets bouncing around. "I gotta see that again!" thinks the child, and launches the next food missile toward the floor. Each new encounter with the food delights the child's senses. But about the time you see it has changed from an accident that entertained to an intentional act, you have had it. Your child holds out his food-covered hands and smiles gleefully. "See what wonderful stuff I've done!" But you overlook the wonderful adventure and go ballistic. "Shame on you. You should know better than to waste your food like that." In that moment there is massive misfit between the baby's expectations (everyone will love this as much as I do) and your reaction.

This rather mundane event—spilling food—becomes a lesson in self-dislike and embarrassment. That often triggers distress and anger, and can escalate to a confrontation between parent and child. When this happens, the whole episode can spiral out of proportion and end up damaging the child and doing a pretty good job of giving the parent a huge headache. In this way, shame is a powerful suppressant of positive emotions and a stimulus for negative ones.

Many parents may recognize a scenario that can happen when you introduce your child to a stranger. It involves not only your child's signals for shame but your own. As Tomkins noted, if a child is shy when presented to a stranger, parents often feel shame themselves. For example, if your child ducks behind you or buries his face in your leg instead of being cute and friendly, you may be inclined to say, "What are you so afraid of? Don't be so unfriendly." And to your friend: "He's usually such an outgoing child. I don't know what's gotten into him." Then, after a while, when your child's feeling of shame eases, he may fix his interest intently on the new person and stare quite openly. You're embarrassed that your child is staring at your friend. You may feel ashamed that your child has no shame. "What are you up to now?" you may say impatiently. Now the little one doesn't know what to do. You've told him over and over to be careful of strangers, and then you've criticized him when he was. And once he's complied with your wish to pay attention to the stranger, you've shamed him for being interested. He clearly can't get anything quite right.

You and your child will be able to have a much more enjoyable time out in the world if you understand what evokes distress in your child and what evokes interest. Then, you may be able to avoid playing the shame card in such situations.

Redirecting Behavior

To reduce the times your child signals shame, consider the following suggestions.

- Try not to use shame as a tool of discipline or punishment. And, as described more fully below, when you do have a problem situation, your goal should be to set limits on the behavior, not to attack the baby's sense of self. In other words, "I love you very much, but you may not climb on that shelf," is a much more productive way of establishing limits than saying, "You are sure a troublemaker, why can't you keep your hands off my things!"
- Use praise, minimize criticism. Praise reinforces good behavior much more effectively than criticism stops bad behavior. A child naturally enjoys being good. Seeing an approving glint in a parent's eye is like oxygen to a child. But when you use shame, it immediately introduces distress, which can easily result in sullenness, anger, rage, and depression.

- Keep the focus on the misdeed or action and not
  the baby's interest or sense of self: "I love you, but
  I'm not happy with this behavior." As a parent you
  will have a much happier child and much more
  peaceful home life if you focus on a child's positive
  attributes and how the mistake might not be
  repeated. For example, you can train your child
  not to make a mess with food without evoking
  shame. "Oh, that is pretty great looking, isn't it?
  But honey, it is really for you to eat. It belongs in
  your mouth, not on the floor. Please don't do that.
  Here's some more milk, keep the cup in your hand
  please! Milk doesn't belong on the floor! If you
  want to play with liquids, we can go to the bathtub
  after you eat." Then you can gently squeeze the
  baby's hand around the cup and move it toward
  his mouth. The child won't learn immediately, but
  that's only natural. If you terrorize the child or
  make the child feel intense shame, you may get
  immediate compliance, but the price you exact is
  too high for such an unimportant result. Kids and
  messes go together, and when you harshly repress
  that impulse you risk constricting exploratory
  learning activities and turning your baby into a
  sullen, frightened child.

How Shame Impacts
All Feelings

Shame can constrict a child's healthy emotional development in
other ways as well. For example, if you admonish your child, "Be
strong. Don't show your feelings. Be brave. Stiff upper lip. What

are you getting all upset about? Don't be a sissy," you are saying in no uncertain terms that she should feel shame for expressing her natural signals. She will be praised for suppressing her feelings.

The effect can be devastating. Not only are you forgetting to validate your child's feelings, but you risk making your child feel that she is out of sync with you, and that can undermine her sense of self and self-esteem.

In his writings, Tomkins provides a moving example of how shame can cause havoc with the entire signaling system. A young boy, Robert, is friendly but somewhat timid. In his playgroup he is often the victim of bullying. It doesn't make him angry; in fact, he is often quite fearful. However, one day when other kids call him chicken for not fighting back, he overcomes his fear and jumps on the bully. A report of his schoolyard scrape gets back to his parents. They are upset and tell him, "Nice little boys don't fight. We're ashamed of you. Whatever got into you? You know better than that!"

Robert starts to cry in distress. The feeling of shame has become too intense to bear. At this point his father scolds him for being such a crybaby. "What are you crying for, just like a baby. Stop it."

The child stops crying and sits down with his family for dinner. The first course is a fruit cup, which he detests. He is disgusted and grimaces, showing his parents just how nauseated the food makes him. This also upsets them and Mother says, "Don't ever make that face again at the table. You don't see us making such expressions, do you?"

Robert hangs his head, waiting for the next course, which is his favorite, roast beef. Suddenly, his excitement over the prospect of getting some food he loves overwhelms him and he reaches across the table to pull a small piece of beef off the serving platter. "I love roast beef," he says.

His father's nostrils flare and he says, "Robert!" with as much disgust and disapproval as he can. Robert lowers his eyes and puts the meat back.

Eventually, after what seems an eternity, he is served some meat. His anticipation of delicious flavor is finally fulfilled and he blurts out, "This is great!"

This time his mother feels duty bound to set him straight about his manners. "Oh, Robert, you'd think you hadn't eaten in a week." His father's eyes reinforce the message. Robert stifles his expression of pleasure and his head drops in shame. After a while his parents notice that their son has slumped down in his chair. His posture reflects his complete surrender to his feelings of shame.

"Robert, where are your manners?" asks his mom. "It's not polite to sit like that at the table." So he sits up, careful to keep his face absolutely expressionless lest he betray any feeling that would displease his parents. Pretty soon they say, "Could you be a bit more attentive? Say something."

This is the last straw. Robert has been instructed that expressions of virtually all signals are, in and of themselves, reason for shame, and now he's told that not being expressive enough is also shameful. Every expression of a signal has been condemned and thwarted. Without meaning to do any harm at all, his parents have set the stage for the possible development of all kinds of emotional turmoil. The outcome of these kinds of assaults on his feelings may lead to distress, chronic rage, and a constriction of interest and enjoyment.

Remember, when children appear to misbehave, everyone ends up happier if parents find ways to turn a potential confrontation into an occasion for redirecting the behavior into interest and enjoyment. For example, I know a world-class physicist whose mom would handle food messes by actually explaining to him what was happening: She'd show her son how the trajectory of the food was a product of certain forces and vectors. They'd even discuss the shape of the splatters. He claims this taught him to understand cause and effect at an early age and allowed him to be curious about how things happen. Perhaps through her clever way of interrupting his problematic behavior, his mom planted the seeds for his later expertise in physics.

The Benefits of Moderating Shame

- Self-esteem grows when shame and humiliation are kept to a minimum.
- Praise, a response that reflects the good in actions, leaves the baby and young child with the sense that his mistakes are not the sum total of him and that it is okay to explore and learn.
- Interest and enjoyment are encouraged.

Disgust and Dissmell

Biologically, dissmell and disgust are . . . responses that have evolved to protect the human being from coming too close to noxious smelling objects and to regurgitate these if they have been ingested.

—Silvan Tomkins, *Affect Imagery Consciousness, Vol. III*

Disgust is signaled by a lowered and protruding lower lip and tongue. A baby or child usually defends himself against noxious flavors by spitting or becoming nauseous and vomiting. Dissmell is signaled by a raised upper lip and nose. A baby or child usually defends himself against noxious odors by turning his head up and to the side and wrinkling his nose. Disgust and dissmell operate on a continuum and are reactions to slightly bad to very bad tastes and smells, respectively.

Brandon was always a happy eater; he was never particularly picky, and since we eat mostly vegetables in our house, he took to them without much problem. But there are two foods he truly hates, tuna fish and mustard. I used to try to get him to taste my tuna sandwich or hot dog with mustard on it, but it would make him so mad at me that I finally gave up. Now that he can talk a little bit, I'm glad I didn't make too big an issue of it. The other day when we were over at a friend's house and they served tuna sandwiches, Brandon turned to me and said, "Mom, that smell makes me want to run away." I laughed and said, "No, we'll make the tuna run away instead," but I thought, how difficult it must be when you are a baby and have really strong opinions about something and can't tell anyone.

—Ruth, thirty-seven, mother
of three-year-old Brandon

DISGUST AND DISSMELL ARE INBORN DEFENSIVE REACTIONS TO unpleasant sensory experiences. You've probably seen these signals many times: Disgust is expressed when your baby slowly spits out the mashed peas you just gave him; dissmell is signaled when your baby turns his head away from the spinach you have offered him.

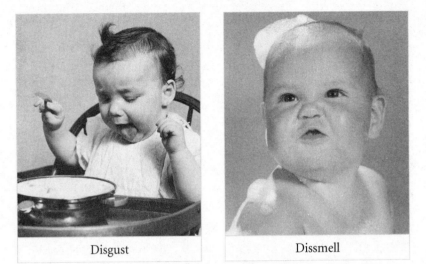

Disgust   Dissmell

A child's expression of disgust and dissmell may not make sense to you—after all, you think the peas taste great and you love the smell of spinach—but you may want to remember that a child's inherent reactions to smell and taste are not whimsical expressions of attitude, they are the result of built-in signals that the child should be allowed to express.

In addition, kids often don't like vegetables because they seem much more pungent and odd tasting than they do to adults. An affection for or tolerance of certain smells and tastes comes with time; you cannot push that biological clock. Over time, children who are exposed to a wide range of foods, presented in a positive light, will often be more adventuresome eaters. Parents who love vegetables are more likely to communicate a positive message about their taste than parents who don't eat them with much gusto. You can try to reintroduce new things, but in ways that aren't forceful. "Just give it one try" is about as adamant as you should be about trying rejected foods.

Think about your own reactions to taste and smell. Your whole adult life people may have been trying to convince you that

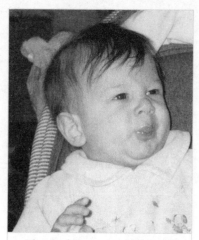

anchovies are delicious, but nothing will ever persuade you that they are anything but disgusting. Whether you are adult or child, taste is something that can be expanded and changed, but only with a person's willing compliance.

By the way, Dr. Seuss's *Green Eggs and Ham* deals with this transition from not liking ("I do not like green eggs and ham") to trying and liking ("I do so like green eggs and ham"). As Dr.

Blend of disgust and dissmell

Michael Basch has noted, the underlying theme of the book is the transition from the signal disgust to the signal of interest. Needless to say, this shift has great importance in areas of learning, prejudice and racism, and so on.

Managing Disgust and Dissmell

As with other signals it is useful to validate the expression of disgust and dissmell, allow their expression and then help ease the cause of your child's aversion. Denying the baby's reaction by saying, "Oh, don't be silly. Bananas are delicious," will bring on other negative reactions—distress and anger, most likely. Contradicting the child's reactions denies her sense of reality and tells her she cannot communicate the current "problem" to you. That erodes her sense of competence. And it puts her on shaky ground when it comes to building the foundation for all kinds of decision making. She needs practice exercising her taste in order to build faith in her own judgments. This helps your child learn to recognize what interests her and brings enjoyment, and to identify what makes her uncomfortable. It is not a stretch to say that emotional honesty and character are built through your baby's ability to accurately know what she likes and doesn't like. So, when it comes to differences of opinions about taste, it is important to recognize and accept your child's separateness and uniqueness. Your tastes and reactions to smells might be different from your child's, but it has no greater meaning or significance than the fact that you have brown hair and your child has blonde hair. In some ways you are and always will be different from one another.

When Signals Turn to Metaphor

When grown-ups say that "a situation stinks" or that some interaction has left "a bad taste in their mouth," they are using the signals for disgust and dissmell symbolically. This translation of taste and smell to psychological expressions of opinion happens slowly. At first, aversion to unpleasant tastes or smells is simply that, but by around one and a half years children attach an opinion to the signal and develop a psychological attachment to their feelings about what is unpleasant or repugnant to them. This process of turning a purely physical signal into an emotional response is an important part of the evolution of a child's emerging capacities for self-reflection, verbalization, and symbolic thinking. That is why it is vital that you continue to listen and pay attention to these signals, allow their expression, validate the feelings, and discuss them. You are helping your child build the foundation for his understanding his internal world of likes and dislikes, interests and disinterests. By listening to the feelings and discussing them, you are enhancing an important decision-making process, helping your child wrestle with what is likable and unlikable, not only in foods and smells but in actions and behaviors in the social world as well.

Interestingly, disgust and dissmell can combine later with other feelings to create more complex psychological states. For example, Tomkins suggested anger combined with dissmell could produce contempt. The expression "looking down one's nose at someone" is a translation of the physical manifestation of dissmell in the infant into a metaphorical attitude of contempt in an adult.

Another way in which your response to these signals influences a child's emerging personality is seen in how some people react to the smell of a dirty diaper, for example. If you make a big deal about how repellant a child's bowel movements are—"Boy, is this a stinker!"—or if you are turned off by your child's normal bodily functions, the child may begin to attach disgust and dissmell to her body and to feel she is personally repellent to the parent. This in turn can result in distress, anger, and shame, with consequences for the child's developing self-confidence. That's why any discussion of disgust and dissmell can lead to consideration of complex issues of likes and dislikes, control, boundaries and separateness, tension regulation, and more.

But even in the simpler area of the relationship of disgust and dissmell to food, parents can have great influence over a child's attitudes. If they create conflicts with their child over the signals for dissmell and disgust, or if they impose their own troubled versions of the signals on the child, they may set the stage for later problems, including tension-regulation difficulties, eating disorders, and so on. Food is a great metaphor for love, comfort, and nurturing: Cravings of various sorts may be addressed with food.

When a child must fight to gain control over his own personal reactions to food, the seeds of later troubles may be sown in unwise battles over food. Again, the basics of dealing with signals apply to the handling of disgust and dissmell: Allow the expression of the signal, validate the signal, and discuss the feelings and the pros and cons of the various options.

Beyond Signals:
When Language Emerges and the Signals Transform into Words

The acquisition of language has a dramatic impact on the child's developing capacity to regulate affects [feelings]. . . . Teaching a child to name feelings and express them in words . . . channels motor behavior into verbal expressiveness, [and] also has a favorable effect on the developing functions of thinking, integration and distinguishing fantasy and wishes from reality.

—Taylor, Bagby, and Parker,
Disorders of Affect Regulation

Verbalization increases . . . the possibility of distinguishing between . . . fantasies . . . and reality. . . . [V]erbalization leads to the integrating process, which in turn results in reality

testing. . . . If the child would verbalize his feelings, he would
learn to delay action.

—Anny Katan, 1961

IT IS DIFFICULT TO OVERESTIMATE THE IMPORTANCE OF HELPING
your child put feelings into words, that is, verbally labeling the
nine signals. Children understand words and ideas long before
they can express them verbally. That's why what you say to and
around an infant can have far-reaching consequences: interesting
word use, patient narration of the passing scene, the absence of
angry or cruel speech, these are all vital to teaching a child how to
use words wisely and effectively to express emotions and ideas.
What children hear becomes the foundation for what they say and
how comfortable they are with words. But it takes them some time
to master the use of words. At first they use them rather crudely.
"Dog" may be used to identify all animals from cat to elephant;
two-word pronouncements such as "No do!" may be used to
express far gentler thoughts like "Please don't make me eat those
peas." In fact, for a child, a no or a command is often the shortest
route to self-expression and these expressions can seem mighty
cantankerous and difficult for a parent to handle. You may find it's
easier to handle the transition to verbal communication with your
child by understanding a bit about how speech arrives, how children use it, and how speech is connected to the nine signals.

How Words Help and Hinder

When a child begins to use words, she may finally be able to provide you with a lot of useful information. At last, she can describe

her feelings of distress or interest more clearly. Words enhance your child's ability to deal with feelings and regulate tension. (This is why I have so strongly emphasized the importance of verbal labeling of the signals.)

In order to fully understand your child's feelings as expressed in words, it is helpful to translate this new vocabulary into signals and feelings, just as you translated the earlier nonverbal facial expressions and gestures into signals and feelings. When you listen to your child's words, ask yourself, what are the signals and feelings behind them? Distress? Anger? Fear? Interest? Enjoyment?

This isn't always easy, however. Many parent-child relationships run into trouble once the child begins to talk. Parents sometimes forget that their child is still expressing the nine basic signals. Now, however, instead of using facial and bodily expressions and nonverbal vocalization, they are using words. And words can mean different things to adults than they do to children—words can also distort, inaccurately label, and deceive. This results in understandable confusion. For adults, words have meanings that have accrued over a lifetime of experiences and feelings. That's one reason parents may automatically try to defend themselves from their child's seemingly critical or harsh words, instead of looking for the underlying intent or meaning as they tried to do with their child's preverbal expressions of signals.

Sometimes, parents take a child's negative statements personally and defensively. This is confusing to the child, who does not know he is wounding you (until your repeated reactions get that message across). Frequently, parents are upset because they think a child who voices distress or anger is "whining" or "acting spoiled" or "disrespecting me."

Not only is this a misinterpretation of what is going on in the child's mind, but by criticizing the expression of distress, the child is made to feel even more misunderstood and becomes even angrier. This is the so-called "double whammy." By repeatedly telling a child that his verbal expressions of the signals for help are a show of bad character ("Don't be such a complainer!"), a parent inhibits the child's expression of emotions. As I have said, this can make the child doubt his own ability to perceive correctly what's going on around him and to react appropriately. When children are repeatedly challenged and criticized for their self-expression they can become distressed, angry, and begin to shut down.

It is natural, and emotionally healthy, for a child to express both positive and negative signals—about her parents, toys, whatever. This is called ambivalence.

When a child says you are the worst parent in the world, he is expressing the negative side of the ambivalence. What he may mean is "I feel ignored, misunderstood, marginalized, thwarted, or confused by something that happened and I need your help in order to feel better." The positive side of the ambivalence— affection, interest, enjoyment—may be right around the corner.

A child's use of words such as "hate" or "no," or phrases such as "no like" or "no do," is simply a way of transmitting one of the negative signals, such as anger, distress, or disgust. And when a parent responds using words such as "whine," "complain," or "disrespect," he is saying he does not like the way the child is expressing the negative signals.

In the throes of such a "conversation," you may want to try to remember that this is a signaling process: The child is trying to convey something about his basic inner feelings. So the key guideline holds: Allow and even encourage expression of all signals, maximize the positive, and address the triggers of the negative.

More Challenges
and Opportunities

"Bad words." Say your increasingly verbal child—whether three, five, or seven years old—blurts out "Damn it!" while struggling to open a cereal box. Rather than automatically jump in with something restrictive like, "That's a bad word—we don't say that here," why not take the opportunity to gather more information from your child about what she is feeling and to really explain to her what you believe about the use of cursing? You might say, "That's interesting. Where did you hear that? In school? From Dad? From Mom?" You also might ask what your child thinks the phrase and words mean. Then you might start a further exchange of information by telling your child what your beliefs are about swearing, using specific words at home or in public, and about conduct that is upsetting to other people. You might keep a dictionary close at hand and use it frequently with your child to look up actual definitions of words that fly out of people's mouths. Such a discussion and explanation conveys a lot of information, creates a dialogue between the two of you, and usually takes the negative charge out of the situation. At the same time, by encouraging a conversation about the incident that prompted the outburst, you can figure out the triggers, discover what may be causing the problem, and help your child solve his dilemma.

Unfortunately, some parents still ascribe to the idea of washing a child's mouth out with soap after she has uttered a "bad" word. There are at least two problems with this approach. First, such actions inflicted on a child will trigger distress, anger, fear, and shame—precisely the negative signals one does not want to elicit when trying to motivate and convey information to the child. Second, what a missed opportunity for learning! The soap message is simply: "Don't say that!" This approach misses a terrific opportunity to define the word, talk about why it might be seen as "bad" or offend others, discuss whether this word should be used in public and by whom, and so on. Such a discussion enhances knowledge and will be understood and accepted far more readily than the soap approach. Next time your child utters a "bad" word, try to "Reach for the dictionary, not the soap!"

Helping your child feel better as she deals with frustration and upset doesn't mean automatically giving in to her demands or allowing her to act out unchecked. By identifying the cause of the upset, allowing the child to voice her distress, and dealing with the trigger, you will cut short the incident and help the child learn that she can gain your help and protection. Over time if you consistently address the cause of the aggressive vocalization, instead of trying to suppress it or stomp it out, your child will learn to modulate how she acts and talks.

The goal for parents is to make the home a safe place for verbal expression of emotions, both positive and negative. If you can let your kids say what and how they feel at home, even when they are angry or critical of you, and then you help them find ways to channel those feelings into well-tempered assertiveness, they will begin to understand themselves better and to have true self-confidence. Then, when they encounter an adverse situation outside the home, they will be better able to control and modulate their responses, to keep their anger to themselves or let it out appropriately.

Why? Why? Why? Another common, and occasionally irksome, result of your child's learning to talk is the nonstop demand that you explain why—why it is time to eat dinner? why is it bad to run into the street? why is it necessary to answer the phone? why is the sky blue? why are you going to work? Why? Why? Why? Although it may sometimes seem to be little more than a relentless demand for attention, in truth, this impulse to question everything is a testimony to the incredible importance of the signal for interest and its role in the intellectual and emotional growth of a young mind. The brain is constantly seeking stimulation; it is essential for its healthy development.

So, when you find yourself dismissing a query with a short, "Because I say so," or "Stop asking so many questions," take a moment to think about how wonderful your child's thirst for interesting information and stimulation really is. This is something to be encouraged, and the payoff is huge: You nurture your child's openness to exploring, learning, and evaluating the world.

Next time your little explorer bombards you, try saying, "That's a dynamite question," or "I'm not sure I know the answer to that . . . let's look it up when we get home." Use dictionaries and maps early and often. These kinds of responses tell your child that you think questions are important to ask and interesting to think about. They help her develop an inclination to learn and to gather and exchange information.

"Shut Up!" What about when your little one first says "shut up" to you? The natural response may be to say: "Don't talk to me like that! We don't use 'shut up' in this house." But, let's step back and unpack what is actually happening here, what feelings are being communicated. When a young child says "shut up," he is telling you he is distressed and probably angry. Why is he feeling this way? More than likely because what is being said to him, the incoming stimulation, is somehow hurtful, overwhelming, and "too much." Whether the child has been criticized, or been asked to clean up his room, or squabbled with his siblings, he has become distressed and angry. He wants to block out the words and lash back and make you feel as he does. Unfortunately, with a "don't say that" response to "shut up," very little information is exchanged and a potentially beneficial process is halted.

So, when the child says "shut up," feelings are being expressed—albeit in a way the parent doesn't like. However, Key #1 (see Chapter 3) focuses on the importance of encouraging the expression of all signals and feelings. In fact, when parents say "don't say that" in response to "shut up," often they are simply responding to a "hot button" from their own childhood, repeating what was done and said to themselves as a child. How can we better handle such a situation?

Actually, this type of situation presents a terrific learning opportunity, for both you and your child. You can start an important process, an exchange of information. You get the chance to learn about what your child is feeling and reacting to, while your child has an opportunity to learn how better to put feelings into words and articulate his responses to distress in a more socially acceptable way.

For instance, when your child says "Oh, shut up," catch yourself and say something like: "Sounds like you're pretty distressed and angry. 'Shut up' doesn't help me understand the problem. Let's talk about it." Then—or perhaps later if everyone needs some time to calm down—you can begin a discussion about what your child is feeling. You might suggest: "Let's see if we can find different words than 'shut up.' I know we can come up with a better way of responding which will explain what's going on." When things are calm, you can discuss the problems associated with saying "shut up" outside as well as inside the home. So, next time your child says "Shut up," how about responding with "Let's talk about it"?

Similarly, here is another story. Your fourth-grade son is asked to write his agenda for the summer months. He writes: "I want to have sex with a girl." Do you freak out? Or tell him to talk with his other parent? Do you say "that kind of thing is inappropriate," in essence, "shut up!"? Or, can you appreciate this as an expression of feeling—be it interest, distress, confusion? By hearing this simply as thoughts and feelings being expressed, not necessarily an intent, you can begin to exchange information. You could ask him to elaborate on his statement, perhaps by asking gently he means what by wanting "to have sex with a girl"? What is sex, anyway? Can we discuss the physiology? And why the addendum "with a girl"? Is he hearing about homosexuality and wanting to talk about that?

The main issue is using this expression of feeling to start a discussion, a process of learning—you from him, and him from you. You are also letting your child know you're available to discuss even the "tough" subjects.

"Mind Your Own Business!" How many of us have often heard—and used—this phrase? Sometimes it is necessary to remind your little ones about boundaries, keeping their hands to themselves and their own things, perhaps especially when siblings are squabbling.

However, "mind your own business" is often blurted out by parents in the face of their child's healthy curiosity. The sequence may go something as follows. The child's interest signal has been triggered; she asks a question; the parent, perhaps feeling a bit caught off balance by the question, or embarrassed, or defensive, shoots back with "mind your own business!" In other words, the parent says: "I don't want to talk with you about that," or "You shouldn't be curious about that," or "I don't like your interest in that topic."

And what happens when the child's interest and curiosity is interfered with? Shame, and an erosion of self-esteem. Moreover, an opportunity for learning is lost. The child is using words to express an interest in something, opening up the possibility for an exchange of information and learning.

Recently, some friends illustrated this dilemma nicely. The

father, a very capable executive who dealt with the finances of a large corporation, was talking with his eleven-year-old daughter. The discussion, as they later told me, moved to family finances, and the daughter began asking questions such as how much money Father made and what the family assets were. "Mind your own business," Father ultimately said, not wanting to talk about it further. What a lost opportunity! Here was the father, with a wonderful chance to begin to share information with and teach his daughter about money, earning money, investments, how to think about money, and so on. And what a teacher the father was—he knew a tremendous amount about money and had important knowledge to convey. Some people are concerned about family privacy in these type of issues, but usually the child will respect requests that certain items not be discussed outside the home. Children's curiosity—interest—about financial matters and about bodily functions frequently stirs up parents' anxieties. But it is almost never too early to start sharing information and helping your child learn about these things, as the onset of her using words will inevitably lead to such questions. An understanding of the signal of interest will enhance your child's learning process and lead you to rethink the "mind your own business" stance.

Understanding the Message Behind Your Child's Words

I wouldn't let my little son ride in the front seat of the car, even for a half-mile, because of the air bags. This sometimes made him angry and he occasionally said, "Oh, Dad, you're so mean." My response was to say, "I love you very much and don't want you to get hurt. If a deer jumps across the road or there is an accident, the air bag can harm you. We don't want that to happen. I have you sit in the backseat because I love you and I care about you." It didn't make him want to ride in the front seat any less, but it did offer him an explanation that provided some soothing. I also tried to talk to him about his underlying message, which was, "You don't think I'm grown up enough to ride in the front seat." I addressed that by saying, "One day you will be bigger and taller than I am. You've already grown up in so many ways, and you'll have the rest of your life to ride in the front seat." That let him know that not only did I understand his frustration and impatience, but there was hope that one day he would be big enough to do what he wanted.

Parents might want to think about what it feels like to be a child, just coming into the power of speech and independent movement. Kids are aware that they are small and don't have control of the world around them. Naturally, until they are grown, they are going to bridle against this inherent reality. As parents, we want them trying to be ever more grown up and independent. In fact, we give them many messages that urge them to behave in adult ways. But they can't always manage the stretch and we often restrain them from particularly adult-like actions for their own safety. From the youngest ages through adolescence, children are caught in this double bind. Parents need to be aware of this fact of life and sensitive to the frustration that it triggers.

How to Help Your Baby
Become an Eager Word User

It's never too soon to introduce your baby to language. From the beginning, listen and talk to your baby at every opportunity—while feeding, changing diapers, or bathing. Sing songs, make nonsense sounds, and talk clearly using adult grown-up language. When your child makes sounds, talk to her about what you think she is saying. During this time her sounds will consist mostly of cooing, fussing, and crying.

In the first months of life you have a chance to introduce your baby to the wonders of sounds and words. From the beginning, your baby will express signals using facial expressions and sounds: various cries communicate hunger, anger, and pain; happy sounds of gurgling, cooing, and babbling convey pleasure. At this time, the baby's main canvas is her own body. She will examine her toes and fingers for hours. For instance, take advantage of her fascination with her own body to name her fingers, feet, knees, nose, as you gently touch them. Also during this time, play off her basic vocal signals and imitate the sounds that baby makes; sing lots of soothing lullabies; play with the baby using toys that make interesting sounds such as rattles; listen to and talk with your baby.

As the child gets older, you have more opportunities to play together and interact. Begin playing peek-a-boo and patty cakes. Don't be shy about using words and actions to interact with your child. You can also introduce the idea of establishing a back and forth dialogue: Hand things to your baby, naming them, and ask the baby to hand them back. At this point, your child's sounds will consist mostly of babbling, including consonant and vowel sounds.

Long before your baby can speak she will understand much of what you say. You can talk to your child about a full range of topics and ideas—don't hold back, thinking she's too young. Ask her questions, explain how things work, talk about what happened yesterday or what you plan for tomorrow. Describe what you see in detail. And give your child a chance to "talk" to you too. Listen to your child, and let her know that what she has to say is important. Patience and imagination may be required to make sense of a toddler's vocabulary but it is important that you encourage the child to talk as often as possible.

Reading favorite books to a child, over and over, may seem boring to an adult, but to a kid it's wonderful fun and helps him learn to use words and eventually to read. This is also a good time to help your child with the concept of give and take—you share ideas, you share words when you play together and have a back and forth conversation.

Speech generally arrives sometime around fifteen to eighteen months, but there is a great developmental variability—it may come earlier or later. As language skills are blossoming, it can be especially valuable to read and tell stories with your baby—pointing to pictures and bringing the words alive with extra facial expressions and exaggerated sounds. Encourage your child to use her blend of baby talk and emerging language to communicate with you. Respond to a baby's chatter by mimicking the sounds and then expanding on their meaning, using language to identify the correct word for objects and actions. During this time communication becomes a hodge-podge of gestures, sounds, and words that are all used to express the nine basic signals of interest, enjoyment, surprise, distress, anger, fear, shame, disgust, and dissmell. Your baby will begin to make two-syllable sounds, such as "dada" and "mama," and respond to simple directions.

As they mature, children are expanding their sense of time and place. During years one to three, you may talk to a child about events that happened in the past or that will happen in the future. Discuss a day's events together. Not only will it help the child expand his vocabulary, but it gives him a chance to communicate his feelings about his time in the playground or at the grocery store. You will learn a lot about his way of looking at the world if you ask questions and listen to the answers.

When Actions Speak

As your child becomes more independent and mobile, she will begin to use overt actions as well as words to express emotions. This newfound ability to express feelings through actions and words makes the signals for help (distress, anger, fear, shame, disgust, and dissmell) seem more aggressive and confrontational. Hitting, spitting, kicking, and even biting can take you by surprise and may seem quite alarming. These actions may have to be contained and stopped, but in the midst of that it is useful to identify and label the signals that the actions are expressing. The challenge is to remember to respond to these signals as you did earlier—by allowing expression of the emotion and at the same time acting promptly to remove the cause of distress and to suggest alternative ways of expressing the feelings.

You can use these times of negative actions as an opportunity to teach your child words that can be used as substitutes for physical acting out. Instead of simply saying, "Don't do that," you might say, "You seem to be angry at me. Is it because I told you that you couldn't have a cookie before dinner?" Labeling and putting words to actions and feelings helps the child make the transition to more mature ways of handling emotion.

Another thought: You may be inclined to ask your child, "Why did you do that?" Sometimes the question may start a useful dialogue, but often it will not get you far. Most of the time kids can't tell you why they did something, because they don't have the self-awareness necessary to answer such a question. Instead, you may have to gently suggest a motive or two and help the child make a connection between a feeling and the words that could be used to explain it.

Reflections on Discipline and Limits

IN A SENSE, MUCH OF THIS BOOK DEALS WITH ISSUES OF DISCIPLINE, limit setting, and providing structure. And—no surprise here—I think you will be able to handle issues of discipline fairly readily if you understand and respond to the signals as I have outlined throughout the book: maximize the signals of fun, attend to the signals of distress, and allow the reasonable expression of all signals.

But so many parents worry about discipline, what constitutes good discipline, and how and when to use it to instruct a child. They may even feel that punishment is the only way to teach a child important life lessons. Often they think that all this attention to a child's signals and the emphasis on encouraging and validating the expression of the signals is somehow spoiling the baby. I can't emphasize enough that discipline involves a process—an ongoing process of tension regulation and learning—rather than something inflicted. This process involves a focus not only on behavior, but on the inner world of feelings. Behaviors are driven by feelings.

You teach self-discipline and awareness of limits best through

231

understanding, interaction, and example, not through punishment. Your beliefs concerning standards of conduct should be reflected in how you conduct yourself and how you treat your child. Kindness, patience, generosity, praise, courtesy (yes, the parent using "please" and "thank you"), acknowledging error, apologizing when appropriate, listening, accepting responsibility, and deferring gratification—these are some of the most important qualities that go into creating a disciplined personality. If you exhibit these qualities, your child will eagerly imitate you and learn these ways of behaving.

This may seem to be a slightly "other" definition of discipline. You may think of discipline as being about enforcing rules and punishing a child when he breaks those rules. But yelling at your child when he makes a scene in a restaurant or cries when he is tired or refuses to share his toys with another infant does not achieve good discipline. And certainly physical punishment does not achieve it. The best discipline is a process of you and your child getting to know her internal world of feelings and tension regulation, and helping her fit her behavior and actions into a social world.

Why Hitting Doesn't Work

Spanking is a euphemism for hitting. Regardless of where on the body the child is hit, hitting is still hitting. If hitting a child is not wrong, then nothing is wrong. Listening to and talking with your child, using words instead of actions, and understanding the feelings behind the behavior—these strategies are far more likely than hitting to result in happy, capable, responsible adults.

Parents who hit (spank) their children have run out of alternatives and are at a loss to communicate using words and examples. They themselves are undisciplined and are teaching their children that there is no reasonable way to handle intense emotions. A household in which physical or verbal abuse is used to enforce behavior can affect a child negatively in several ways. It may make the child fearful, withdrawn, and unsure of himself. Or it may produce a bully who imitates the parent's behavior and in turn picks on weaker children and asserts his own need for power and control on others through unpleasant and antisocial acts. But, however your child reacts to "strict" discipline, you can be sure it is not in a way that helps the child become the best person he or she would be.

Many problems can occur when you hit or yell at your child. First, you may evoke your child's tendency to identify with you and your behavior. This means that because your child wants to be like you, if you hit or yell at him, he may mimic your behavior and respond similarly in similar circumstances. Children often do what is done to them.

Second, if you physically punish a child, the child may think that hitting is the appropriate response to most external challenges or internal upsets such as frustration, anger, fear, or shame.

Third, hitting creates an emphasis on actions instead of on well-chosen and expressive words. Learning to turn actions into the rational expression of words is a very important part of healthy emotional development. It helps the brain put various feelings and frustrations into symbols—words—rather than actions or uncontrolled outbursts. Using words to express intense feelings allows your child to realize there are many different ways to handle self-expression and to manage emotions and allows your child's brain to become more agile in adapting to various situations. Occasionally, of course, words and ideas need to be put into actions in order to make a point or make things happen. More usually with infants and children, however, you want to show them how to translate actions and impulsivity into expressive, appropriate words.

A much more effective and healthy alternative to hitting (or yelling at) your child is to help your child develop discipline by teaching him what is appropriate behavior and what is not; by helping him understand how to control his impulses and how to accept delayed gratification; and by helping him develop a solid sense of himself (a particularly useful trait when he becomes a teenager—it will help him resist negative peer pressure and destructive temptations).

Figuring out how to do all that is not always easy, but it relies on the same principles that guide your responses to a child's signals. Again, the basics include: encouraging the expression of the signals; maximizing the signals of fun; attending to the causes of the signals for help; and keeping an eye on your own verbalizations and behavior, because your child sure is. These basics can be stated in many different ways, and enhanced by other tricks. For example, remember that praise will work better than criticism, so make a real effort to encourage good behavior. Look for the triggers (tired, hungry, in pain) of "bad" behavior and attend to them. And nurture your child's self-esteem and self-confidence by paying attention to his feelings and respecting them.

When "No!" Means No

Your goal is to teach through example and understanding, not punishment, but sometimes you have to act swiftly and protect your child. When your impulsive child heads for the street, the immediate issue is urgent. But even in such life or death matters, you need to make wise choices about how you communicate "Don't run into the street" and what you say afterwards. Terror can enforce behavior, but it cannot produce a child who learns to have confidence in his or her own decision-making abilities— an essential foundation for self-discipline. Fear alone does not help a child begin to sort out which interesting stimuli are dangerous, which are not, and why. I suggest that even with a young child, after you take the child from harm's way and things have calmed down, you offer an explanation for your actions: "It's dangerous to go into the street. You can get hurt badly and I don't ever want that to happen to you. I got angry because I was scared you would be hurt. Streets and cars are interesting but they can be very dangerous . . . they can hurt you." You will get better results, and a child will be better able to make responsible decisions about his own safety, if you talk and listen instead of yell, and use words instead of harsh actions, in communicating the message.

When You're at
Your Wit's End

About the fourth time your child pulls everything out of the cupboards, despite your admonitions to stop, you probably feel like swatting his little hand, putting him in the crib, or at least shouting. But try to think again. Infants and young children are not simply being bad when they act up. A lot is going on in those kinds of situations. Children do not know that expressing interest in a book by looking at it is substantially different than expressing interest in a book by ripping out the pages. They will gain the capacity for impulse control only slowly—and much of the success of this process depends on your own impulse control. They are willful; they are uninformed. They are trying to find out who they are and how they fit into the world. They experiment with testing boundaries. They are interested in provoking your responses just to see what they will be. So, while you may want to inform your cupboard-trashing child of your rules and advocate that he curbs his willfulness, merely scolding him or shouting out directives may not be the most effective way to teach a child right from wrong or good actions from bad.

The key is to allow the signals for interest and enjoyment to be expressed while you show the child alternative ways of expressing those signals. If your child begins tearing at the book's pages you might say, "I know tearing pages is fun—neat noise, making many things out of one thing . . . but we can't tear this book, let's put it away until we can read it properly. Here, let's play with this sheet of colored paper instead. I'll put the book away for later when we feel like reading." If you come into the room and see that the book is already destroyed, it's too late to intervene. If you yell, the child will have little or no idea what you're so worked up about. The truth is if you leave a child unattended, stuff is going to happen and not all of it will make you happy. Is that the child's fault? Not necessarily. Her brain is doing just what it is wired to do: seek out interesting stimuli. If the book is torn up while you are out of the room, one way to effectively establish discipline is to say, "Oh my, look at the book. Now we won't be able to read it because the pages are ripped out. This kind of book is to be read, not to have the pages ripped out. I'll let you have a reading book when you can use it properly. Next time you feel like playing with paper, let's use your drawing pad." The brain does better with more information. Even a child who cannot quite comprehend all the words will understand the gist and emotions of what you are saying, and as your child becomes able to understand you, she will accept that you are suggesting alternative behaviors.

You're Skeptical?

I can hear parents saying, "Yeah, but what about a really willful kid; one that is constantly making a mess or repeatedly doing things you've asked them not to do, or getting angry over nothing?" True, some kids are more temperamental than others; some seem less able to accept frustration; some are ferocious about doing what they want when they want to. But, by and large, children express emotions in response to stimulation—that is, to something inside or outside of themselves. For example, fussiness and bad temper are associated with the signals for distress and anger. If your child is in the middle of an angry outburst that you feel needs limits, ask yourself, "Is he hungry? tired? sick? bored?" If you can say yes to any one of those, it makes sense to take care of that problem. Food, sleep, TLC, or something interesting rather than punishment are needed, and will probably resolve the problem.

Another concern that some parents express regarding this focus on understanding instead of punishment is that it may make a child spoiled or weak. Parents who feel this way think they have the child's best interest at heart. They are not mean (not intentionally), they are just passing along their sense of how the world is set up and what it takes to get along in it. But I believe they are making a mistake. The world will dish out its quota of hard knocks to your child soon enough; there's no avoiding it. Why make that happen sooner rather than later? Children who are well loved and are treated with understanding, patience, and compassion tend to have better tension regulation, are less defensive and more resilient than children who are harshly punished for their infractions of house rules. They are *better* able to deal with life's surprises and difficulties, not less.

Do You Need More Insight, Too?

If your child is always acting out, defying your edicts, just cruising for trouble, you might ask yourself: "What am I doing to contribute to my child's distress and anger? Am I impatient, impulsive, self-centered—the very things I'm accusing my child of? Am I misunderstanding something important that my child is trying to tell me?" And if you let your child know you are self-questioning and introspective—preverbal kids can pick this up from your actions and your words—your child will identify with this process and have a greater ability to ask herself, "What am I, the child, doing to contribute to the upset?" This is exactly what you want to happen, for then your child becomes part of the solution, gaining the ability to be introspective and regulate tension.

Using Rewards to Enhance Structure

The concept of rewarding good behavior is controversial to some parents and experts. But I have found it can be applied wisely and effectively. If a child marks on your carpet with a pen, you might take the pen away, explaining, "I think you cannot use the pen again until you can use it properly." "Pens are usually for writing on paper, not carpets or walls. We'll get the pen out when you can use it properly." Using a reward system, you might even say: "Thank you for not marking more than you did on the carpet . . . Thank you for not drawing on the walls." This praise goes a long way. After all, the gleam in your eye is terrific motivation for your child. When the child learns, he is rewarded with the pen and paper. This is quite different from saying, "You are a bad child. Go to your room." With the latter response there's a good chance you and your child will get caught up in an escalating exchange of angry emotions, with little learned.

Epilogue

As Your Child Gets Older . . .

We can succeed only by concert. It is not "can any of us imag-ine better?" but, "can we all do better?" . . . Object whatso-ever is possible, still the question recurs, "can we do better?"

—Abraham Lincoln, 1862,
Annual Message to Congress

THIS BOOK IS COMING TO AN END, BUT YOUR CHILD'S LIFE IS JUST beginning. The signals and emotions I've described form the foundation of her emotional life. If you understand a bit about this foundation, this embryology of feelings, everything else pretty much falls into place. But, I can hear parents asking, what about after the preverbal years? What about toddlerhood, later childhood, adolescence, young adulthood, adulthood? What about your child's career choice, finding a spouse, having chil-dren?

It turns out the same guidelines apply to all these develop-

239

mental stages. Keep doing what you are doing. Don't lose sight of the basics—the signals, which are the foundation of feelings. Encourage the expression of the feelings. Focus on interest and enjoyment. Take care of whatever triggers the negative signals such as distress or anger. And continue putting all of this into words.

Your baby brings a lot into the world in terms of her genetic code. But you—her parents—and the rest of the environment also exert a tremendous influence on your baby's development through your interactions with her. Today's child development researchers have shown that your child uses the nine basic signals we have been discussing throughout this book to interact with you and the world at large. These nine signals comprise a child's earliest feelings, and the interactions with you and others are what allow a child to establish her basic emotional life.

A lot happens during the preverbal months and years—and a lot happens afterwards as well. Throughout our lives there is, as Nobelist Gerald Edelman points out, a dynamic fluidity in our brain. However, the earliest years seem to have special impact on many of our most basic emotional and behavioral patterns, patterns that lie beyond our conscious awareness. John Gedo is a preeminent psychoanalyst who has closely watched the contributions of biology to human psychology. He has shown how many aspects of character, actions, habits, mood, tension regulation, and so on involve early patterns of which we have no conscious memory. These early patterns stem from the infant's genetic endowment in concert with the early parent-infant interactions around the basic signals.

We have talked throughout this book about preventing emotional and behavioral problems. How? By understanding the signals at all ages, whether conveyed preverbally or verbally, by facial expressions or words, and responding reasonably to them. And we have talked about enhancing potential. How? By realizing the brain is stimulus-seeking and that the goal is to open up options and encourage learning rather than constrict the child's internal emotions and inhibit thinking, acting, and feeling through the use of fear and shame.

The early years of infancy and childhood would appear, then, to provide a real opportunity to get your child off to a good start—to enhance potential and prevent problems. The guidelines described here are easy to follow and are based on the nine signals—the foundation of a child's emotional life. Encourage the expression of feelings; focus on the positive signals of interest and enjoyment; and attend to the triggers of negative signals. And not only are the guidelines easy once one understands the foundation . . . but you can use them in all the decades to come. Good luck, and have fun!

Appendices

A Guide to Further Insights

In this book I have attempted to highlight and integrate a variety of key issues from the recent explosion in scientific work on infant and child development. In my opinion, the most important of these topics involves affect theory, that is, what emotions are and how they develop and function. Why is this so important? Because affects provide the foundation for so much of the rest of human development, such as attachment, relationships, personality development, psychopathology, cognitive and intellectual development, and so on. The bulk of this book represents an attempt to describe these affects, or signals, show how they work, and convey various implications for raising children and preventing psychopathology. This appendix goes into more detail with respect to the history and technical aspects of affect theory; it leans heavily upon the work of Silvan Tomkins and his colleagues. Tomkins, a psychologist, worked during the second half of the twentieth century; his academic affiliations include Harvard and Princeton.

A Brief History of Affect Theory

A detailed historical review of affects is beyond our scope here, but some trends might be noted in order to provide a general context. About 140 years ago, in 1862, the French neurologist Duchenne published his detailed mapping of facial muscle response to electrical stimulation. Darwin, in his 1872 work *The Expression of the Emotions in Man and Animals,* was influenced by and used many of Duchenne's findings. Darwin concluded that certain facial expressions were inherited and had evolved ultimately into a signaling system. By 1915, Freud considered affect to be conscious manifestation of instinct, the qualitative transformation of instinctual energy. Later, as he struggled with his understanding of anxiety, affect became a communication and part of an internal feedback system rather than an indicator of discharge (Freud, 1926, 1933; Basch, 1976). Subsequently, many prominent theoreticians, clinicians, and researchers (e.g., Basch, Demos, Emde, Gedo, Kernberg, Krystal, Lichtenberg, Parens, Shevrin, Stern, and many others) have focused on various aspects of affects. The data they compiled included clinical cases and studies, anatomical work, electromyography, high-speed films, patients with neurological lesions permitting the description of the facial musculature and autonomic nervous system, various types of brain imagings and scans, and so on.

In the early 1960s, Tomkins began publishing his detailed studies. He defined affect as innate biological (universal) responses to various stimuli, with these responses being manifested in the skin, vocal apparatus, musculature, and autonomic system, particularly in the facial region. In his initial publications in 1962 and 1963 he distinguished eight affects: interest, enjoyment, surprise, distress, anger, fear, shame, and disgust (disgust is reaction to noxious tastes). These eight affects were seen as operating on a continuum from low to high: interest-to-excitement; enjoyment-to-joy; surprise-to-startle; distress-to-anguish; anger-to-rage; fear-to-terror; shame-to-humiliation; and contempt-to-disgust. Some thirty years later, in works published just prior to his death in 1991 as well as posthumously, Tomkins made several revisions, including distinguishing nine rather than eight affects.

He separated out disgust and dissmell (dissmell, a neologism for which Tomkins apologized, is a reaction to noxious odors) as distinct innate patterns of reaction; and he deleted contempt, which he suggested was a later learned amalgam of anger and dissmell.

His final list of innate affects, then, included two positive affects (interest-to-excitement, enjoyment-to-joy), one resetting affect clearing the nervous system (surprise-to-startle), and six negative affects (distress-to-anguish; anger-to-rage; fear-to-terror; shame-to-humiliation; disgust; dissmell).

Many important works were published during the 1990s that highlighted the neurobiological aspects of affect as well as the evolution of the role of affect in clinical and theoretical advances. For example, *Disorders of Affect Regulation* (by Taylor, Bagby, and Parker), Schore's *Affect Regulation and the Origin of the Self: The Neurobiology of Emotional Development,* Plutchik's *The Psychology and Biology of Emotion,* and Panksepp's *Affective Neuroscience: The Foundations of Human and Animal Emotions* are marvelous treatises on the complex interactions between genetic, neurobiologic, and environmental factors in emotional development. John Gedo's *The Evolution of Psychoanalysis: Contemporary Theory and Practice* is a brilliant description of changes in clinical work and theory over the past century. He also highlights how enhanced understanding of the neurological and psychological aspects of affects contributes greatly to these advances.

The Full Scope of the Signals

Affects, or signals, are universal, inborn biological responses to various stimuli—they have been found in all cultures thus far studied. These early signals represent the embryology of our later feelings and emotions, as they make the complex transformation from the biological to the psychological. Although there is ongoing scientific debate regarding the number and time of emergence of affects, most current research suggests we are born with approximately nine basic affects: interest, enjoyment, surprise, distress, anger, fear, shame, disgust, and dissmell. The fact that there are more negative than positive affects appears to be an evolutionary phenomenon: It is more important for the survival of the organism to be able to signal when it is in trouble than when it is not.

Throughout this book I have focused on the role the affect system plays in communication. I have also stressed the importance of this communication system for the interactions between the infant/child and caregiver, which lead to the development of the internal tension-regulation capacities of the child. However, in addition to providing communication, this complex affect system also appears to serve as our major source of motivating feedback. Affect seems to create a sense of urgency which is experienced as motivating and which primes the organism to act. Tomkins argued that affect is the primary motivating system, acting as a general amplifier for drives, cognition, perception, and action. Tomkins went so far as to suggest that affects evolved primarily as motivators, with communication being a secondary spin-off.

Tomkins also discussed affects as motivators in humans by postulating four principles, or what he called *general images:* positive affect should be maximized; negative affect should be minimized; affect inhibition should be minimized; and power to maximize positive affect, to minimize negative affect, and to minimize affect inhibition should be maximized. Throughout this book, I have utilized these general images somewhat differently from Tomkins and tried to highlight the potential of these ideas in the area of prevention. Interestingly, early prevention programs and effective clinical work with patients demonstrate patterns quite consistent with these principles.

How do affects seem to work? The studies noted above explore various data and hypotheses involving neurological patterns and locations in the brain. Tomkins suggested that differences in affect activation are accounted for by three variants of a single principle, namely, the density of neural firing (density referring to frequency of neural firing per unit time). The three variants are stimulus increase, stimulus level, and stimulus decrease (see Figures 1–3 on pages 252–54). For example, any stimulus (light, sound, etc.) with a relatively sudden onset and a steep increase in the rate of neural firing will innately activate a surprise-to-startle response; if the rate of neural firing increases less rapidly, fear is activated; and if still less rapidly, then interest is innately activated. In contrast, any sustained increase in the level of neural firing (such as a continuing loud noise) would innately activate the cry of distress; if it were sustained and still louder, it would activate the anger responses. Any sudden decrease in stimulation would innately activate the smile of enjoyment.

The affects shame-to-humiliation and disgust and dissmell are a bit different. With respect to the former, shame may manifest somewhat later than the other affects, when interpersonal validation of the baby's behavior becomes increasingly important. Shame involves the absence of a confirming response, leading to an inadequate reduction of excitement and a shame reaction. Shame is termed an affect auxiliary and is specifically related to other affects: shame operates only after the affects of interest and/or enjoyment have been activated—it impedes one or the other or both. In addition, shame, shyness, guilt, and discouragement may be identical as affects, although they are experienced differently because of perceived causes and consequences. Shame is about inferiority; shyness is about strangeness of the other; guilt is about moral transgression; and discouragement is about temporary defeat. But Tomkins suggests that the core affect in all four is identical. Shame also appears intimately related to self-esteem. Many clinicians suggest the development of a healthy sense of self and self-esteem involves validation of the positive affects of interest and enjoyment and concepts of competency. The inappropriate and excessive use of shame thus erodes self-esteem inasmuch as it interferes with the positive affects.

Disgust and dissmell are considered to be innate defensive responses; they are termed *drive auxiliaries,* with their function being to protect human organisms from noxious and dangerous foods and odors. Disgust is related to taste and the gastrointestinal system; nausea and vomiting can be elicited to help rid the body of dangerous substances. Dissmell involves the olfactory system, with the typical evasive maneuvers visible in infancy. The early warning response via the nose is dissmell; the next level of response, from the mouth or stomach, is disgust. Later, these affects psychologically are related to rejection and contempt. Such phrases as "this leaves a bad taste in my mouth" or "this has a bad smell to it" convey the link between the physiological affects of disgust/dissmell and psychological rejection and contempt.

It is interesting (and of clinical significance) to note that affects themselves interact in various ways and can themselves be innate activators of other affects. For example, anger can be triggered by excessive distress as well as by an excess of any of the other negative affects, such as fear or shame, and interruption of interest can lead to distress and then anger.

Which signals tend to be seen earliest and in what situation? Interest, enjoyment, surprise, distress, and fear can readily be seen in the first several months. Distress-to-anguish tends to predominate early on, and initially this signal involves the various physical needs of the baby: pain, fatigue, hunger, temperature, and so on. Some have suggested understimulation-to-boredom as an affect. Although others disagree, an understanding of boredom as a counterpart to interest-to-excitement is crucial. Similarly, some have seen sadness as a separate affect. Tomkins and others consider sadness as a derivative of distress. What about anxiety? Anxiety has a long and complicated theoretical history. Tomkins concluded that anxiety was most accurately regarded as the fear-to-terror affect, regardless of whether the object is known or not, internal or external, conscious or unconscious.

The Transformation from the Biological to the Psychological

The problem of the transformation of, and relationship between, the biological and psychological is intriguing, with a variety of proposals to consider. This involves the development of affect throughout infancy and childhood. This complicated topic warrants a separate work, and would include such issues as consciousness and unconsciousness, the neurophysiology involved, how awareness of internal subjective states occurs, and so on.

Michael Basch suggested reserving the term "affect" for the group of biological reactions to stimulation described by Tomkins; "feeling," then, refers to those reactions being related to a concept of the self (around eighteen to twenty-four months); "emotion" results when feeling states are joined with experience to give personal meaning to complex concepts such as love, hate, and happiness (about four to six years); "empathic understanding" then represents the final transformation of affective development (around eleven to twelve years), when affective communication goes beyond the self-referential.

In his book *The Interpersonal World of the Infant* Stern seemed to be struggling with this transformation when he described representations of interactions that have been generalized (RIGs). He began by using the term *episode* for the basic unit of memory. Several specific episodes then made up the *generalized episode*—a structure about the likely course of events, based on average experiences. Accordingly, the generalized episode creates expectations of actions, of feelings, of sensations, and so on that can either be met or violated. Stern suggested that these episodes are averaged and represented preverbally: they become RIGs.

Lane and Schwartz in their article "Levels of emotional awareness: a cognitive-developmental theory and its application to psychopathology" conceptualized a cognitive development model for understanding the organization of emotional experience. They integrated Piaget's theory of cognitive development with ideas about symbolization and language development. Their model has five levels of emotion organization and awareness: (1) sensorimotor reflexive (emotion is experienced only as bodily sensations, but may be evident to others in the individual's facial expression); (2) sensorimotor enactive (emotion is experienced as both a body sensation and an action tendency); (3) preoperational (emotions are experienced psychologically as well as somatically, but they are unidimensional and verbal descriptions are often stereotyped); (4) concrete operational (there is an awareness of blends of feelings and the individual can describe complex and differentiated emotional states that are part of his or her subjective experience); and (5) formal operational (there is an awareness of combinations of blends of feelings, as well as a capacity to make subtle distinctions between nuances of emotion, and an ability to comprehend the multidimensional emotional experience of other people).

Tomkins appeared to use script theory to account for the transformation to the symbolic and learned: "In script theory, I define the scene as the basic element in life as it is lived. . . . [It] includes at least one affect and at least one object of that affect"—the object is not necessarily a person, and may even be another affect. Connecting one affect-laden scene with another affect-laden scene involves the formation of scripts. "The script," Tomkins says, deals with the "individual's rules for predicting, interpreting, responding to, and controlling a magnified set of scenes." Cognition is then seen as providing psychological magnification, that is, connecting one affect-laden scene with another. Psychological magnification is a phenomenon provided by cognition, with cognition referring to the organization of memory, perception, action, and affect. Thus Tomkins attempted to account for how stimuli which are learned or have "meaning" can themselves trigger affects. In addition, it is through the utilization of script theory that Tomkins explored in great detail issues such as structure formation and personality characteristics. This sequence involving scenes and scripts is similar to Stern's concept of RIGs.

This, then, concludes a brief technical summary on affect theory. Much has been written about affect by many researchers, and an expansion of the views above as well as other perspectives can be found throughout the bibliography. Virginia Demos has suggested that Tomkins and his colleagues have presented us with a current "state of the art" theory of the workings of affect. Doubtless the following years will see enhancements in our understanding of these important processes. Yet, for the moment, this confluence of ideas at the beginning of the twenty-first century appears to give us a major opportunity to understand human emotions and behavior and to enhance the potential of and help prevent problems in our children.

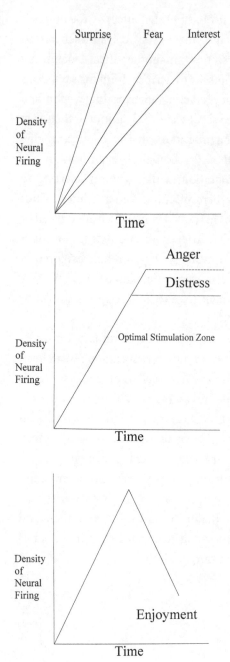

Figure 1.
Surprise, fear, and interest.

Any stimulus with a relatively sudden onset and a steep increase in the rate of neural firing will innately activate *surprise*. If the rate of neural firing increases less rapidly, *fear* is activated. If the rate increases still less rapidly, *interest* is innately activated.

Figure 2.
Distress and anger.

Any sustained increase in the level of neural firing, such as a continuing loud noise, innately activates the cry of *distress*. If it were sustained and still louder, if would innately activate the *anger* response.

Figure 3.
Enjoyment.

Any sudden decrease in stimulation which reduced the rate of neural firing, as in the sudden reduction of excessive noise, would activate the smile of *enjoyment*.

Resources

Als, Heidi. "A syntactive model of neonatal behavioral organization." *Physical and Occupational Therapy in Pediatrics* 6(1986):3–55.

Altshul, Saul. *Childhood Bereavement and Its Aftermath.* Madison, CT: International Universities Press, 1988.

Barnard, Kathryn, Colleen Morisset, and Susan Spieker. "Preventive intervention: enhancing parent-infant relationships." In *Handbook of Infant Mental Health,* edited by C. H. Zeanah. New York: Guilford, 1993, pp. 386–401.

Basch, Michael F. "The concept of affect: A re-examination." *Journal of the American Psychoanalytic Association* 24(1976):759–77.

———. *Understanding Psychotherapy: The Science Behind the Art.* New York: Basic Books, 1988.

Benedek, Therese. "Parenthood as a developmental phase." *Journal of the American Psychoanalytic Association* 7(1959):389–417.

Brazelton, T. Berry, and Stanley I. Greenspan. *The Irreducible Needs of Children.* Cambridge, MA: Perseus Publishing, 2000.

Campbell, S. B. "Behavior problems in preschool children: A review of recent research." *Journal of Child Psychology and Psychiatry* 36(1995):113–49.

Cohen, Lawrence J. *Playful Parenting.* New York: Ballantine Books, 2001.

Crittenden, P. M. "Peering into the black box: An exploratory treatise on the development of self in young children." In *Rochester Symposium on Developmental Psychopathology,* edited by Dante Cicchetti and Sheree Toth. Vol. 5, *Disorders and Dysfunctions of the Self.* Rochester, NY: University of Rochester Press, 1994, pp. 79–148.

Darwin, Charles. *The Expression of the Emotions in Man and Animals.* Chicago: University of Chicago Press, 1965 (1872).

Demos, E. Virginia. "Differentiating the repetition compulsion from trauma through the lens of Tomkins' script theory: A response to Russell." In *Trauma, Repetition, and Affect Regulation: The Work of Paul Russell,* edited by Judith Ginn Teicholz and Daniel Kriegman. New York: Other Press, 1998, pp. 67–104.

———. "Empathy and Affect: Reflections on infant experience." In *Empathy II,* edited by J. Lichtenberg, M. Bornstein, and D. Silver. New Jersey: The Analytic Press, 1984, pp. 9–34.

———. *Exploring Affect: The Selected Writings of Silvan S. Tomkins.* Cambridge, Eng.: Cambridge University Press, 1995.

———. "Links between mother-infant transactions and the infant's psychic organization." Paper presented to the Chicago Psychoanalytic Society, Chicago, May 1994.

————. "Facial expressions of infants and toddlers: A descriptive analysis." In *Emotion and Early Interaction*, edited by T. Field and A. Fogel. Hillsdale, NJ: Laurence Erlbaum, 1982, pp. 127–60.

Denham, Susanne A. *Emotional Development in Young Children*. New York: Guilford Press, 1998.

Dunn, J. *From One Child to Two*. New York: Fawcett Columbine, 1995.

Edelman, Gerald. *Bright Air, Brilliant Fire*. New York: Basic Books, 1992.

Ekman, Paul, ed. *Darwin and Facial Expression*. New York and London: Academic Press, 1973.

————. *The Expression of the Emotions in Man and Animals*, by Charles Darwin. New York: Oxford University Press, 1998. (Original work published in 1872.)

Fajardo, Barbara. "Constitution in infancy." *Progress in Self Psychology* 4(1988):91–109.

Fonagy, Peter, György Gergely, Elliott Jurist, and Mary Target. *Affect Regulation, Mentalization, and the Development of the Self*. New York: Other Press, 2002.

Fraiberg, Selma. *The Magic Years*. New York: Scribner, 1959.

Fraiberg, Selma, ed. *Clinical Studies in Infant Mental Health*. New York: Basic Books, 1980.

Fraiberg, Selma, E. Adelson, and V. Shapiro. "Ghosts in the nursery: A psychoanalytic approach to the problems of impaired infant-mother relationships." *Journal of the American Academy of Child Psychiatry* 14(1975):387–421.

Free, K., I. Alechina, and C. Zahn-Waxler. "Affective language between depressed mothers and their children: The potential impact of psychotherapy." *Journal of the American Academy of Child and Adolescent Psychiatry* 35(1996):783–90.

Freud, Sigmund. *The Unconscious*. Standard Edition 14. London: Hogarth Press, 1915, 166–204.

————. *Inhibitions, Symptoms and Anxiety*. Standard Edition 20. London: Hogarth Press, 1926.

————. *New Introductory Lectures on Psycho-analysis*. Standard Edition 22. London: Hogarth Press, 1933.

Furman, E. "On feeling and being felt with." *Psychoanalytic Study of the Child* 47(1992):67–84.

Gaddini, Eugenio. "On imitation." *International Journal of Psycho-Analysis* 50(1969): 475–84.

————. "Early defensive fantasies and the analytic process." *International Journal of Psycho-Analysis* 63(1982):379–88.

Gedo, John E. *The Evolution of Psychoanalysis: Contemporary Theory and Practice*. New York: Other Press, 1999.

George, M. S., T. A. Ketter, P. Parekh, B. Horowitz, P. Herscovitch, and R. M. Post. "Brain activity during transient sadness and happiness in healthy women." *American Journal of Psychiatry* 152(1995):341–51.

Goodfriend, Marlene. "Treatment of attachment disorder of infancy in a neonatal intensive care unit." *Pediatrics* 91(1993):139–52.

Gopnik, A., and A. N. Meltzoff. "Imitation, cultural learning and the origins of 'theory of mind.'" *Behavioral and Brain Sciences* 16(1993):521–22.

Greenspan, Stanley I. *Developmentally Based Psychotherapy.* Madison, CT: International Universities Press, 1997.

———. *Infancy and Early Childhood: The Practice of Clinical Assessment and Intervention with Emotional and Developmental Challenges.* Madison, CT: International Universities Press, 1992.

Greenspan, S. I., and N. T. Greenspan. *The Emotional Partnership.* New York: Viking, 1989.

Gross, Deborah, Louis Fogg, and Sharon Tucker. "The efficacy of parent training for promoting positive parent-toddler relationships." *Research in Nursing and Health* 18(1995):489–99.

Hadley, June L. "Attention, affect, and attachment." *Psychoanalysis and Contemporary Thought* 8(1985):529–50.

———. "The neurobiology of motivational systems." In *Psychoanalysis and Motivation,* edited by Joseph D. Lichtenberg. Hillsdale, NJ: Analytic Press, 1989, pp. 337–72.

Harris, Irving B. *Children in Jeopardy: Can We Break the Cycle of Poverty?* New Haven: Yale University Press, 1996.

Holinger, Paul C. "Early intervention and prevention of psychopathology: The potential role of affect." *Clinical Social Work Journal* 28(2000):23–41.

———. "A developmental perspective on psychotherapy and psychoanalysis." *American Journal of Psychiatry* 146(1989):1404–12.

———. *Violent Deaths in the United States: An Epidemiologic Study of Suicide, Homicide, and Accidents.* New York: Guilford Press, 1987.

Holinger, Paul C., Daniel Offer, James T. Barter, and Carl C. Bell. *Suicide and Homicide Among Adolescents.* New York: Guilford Press, 1994.

Hurn, Hal. "Synergic relations between the processes of fatherhood and psychoanalysis." *Journal of the American Psychoanalytic Association* 17(1969):437–51.

Izard, Carroll E. *The Face of Emotion.* New York: Appleton-Century-Crofts, 1971.

Johnson, M. K., and K. S. Multhaup. "Emotion and MEM." In *The Handbook of Emotion and Memory: Research and Theory,* edited by S.-A. Christianson. Hillsdale, NJ: Lawrence Erlbaum, 1992, pp. 33–66.

Katan, Anny. "Some thoughts about the role of verbalization in early childhood." *Psychoanalytic Study of the Child* 16(1961):184–88.

Kitzman, H., D. L. Olds, C. R. Henderson, C. Hanks, R. Cole, R. Tatelbaum, K. M. McConnochie, K. Sidora, D. W. Luckey, D. Shaver, K. Englehardt, D. James, and K. Barnard. "Effect of prenatal and infancy home visitation by nurses on pregnancy outcomes, childhood injuries, and repeated childbearing." *Journal of the American Medical Association* 278(1997):644–52.

Kohut, Heinz. *The Analysis of the Self.* New York: International Universities Press, 1971.

Krause, Rainer. Book review of *Affect Imagery Consciousness: Volume III* by Silvan S. Tomkins in *Journal of the American Psychoanalytic Association* 43(1995):929–38.

Krystal, Henry. *Integration and Self-Healing: Affect, Trauma, and Alexithymia.* Hillsdale, NJ: Analytic Press, 1988.

Kumin, Ivri. *Pre-Object Relatedness: Early Attachment and the Psychoanalytic Situation.* New York: Guilford Press, 1996.

Lane, Richard D., Eric M. Reiman, Geoffrey L. Ahern, Gary E. Schwartz, and Richard J. Davidson. "Neuroanatomical correlates of happiness, sadness, and disgust." *American Journal of Psychiatry* 154(1997):926–33.

Lane, Richard, and Gary Schwartz. "Levels of emotional awareness: a cognitive-developmental theory and its application to psychopathology." *American Journal of Psychiatry* 144(1987):133–43.

Levin, Fred. *Mapping the Mind.* Madison, CT: International Universities Press, 1991.

Lieberman, Alicia F., and Jeree H. Pawl. "Infant-parent psychotherapy." In *Handbook of Infant Mental Health,* edited by Charles H. Zeanah. New York: Guilford Press, 1993, pp. 427–42.

Lieberman, Alicia F. *The Emotional Life of the Toddler.* New York: Free Press, 1993.

Meisels, S. J., M. Dichtelmiller, and F. R. Liaw. "A multi-dimensional analysis of early childhood intervention programs." In *Handbook of Infant Mental Health,* edited by Charles H. Zeanah. New York: Guilford Press, 1993, pp. 361–85.

Meltzoff, Alexander N. "Foundations for developing a concept of self: The role of imitation in relating self to others and the value of social mirroring, social modeling, and self-practice in infancy." In *The Self in Transition: Infancy to Childhood,* edited by D. Ciccetti and M. Beeghly. Chicago: University of Chicago Press, 1990, pp. 139–64.

Nathanson, Donald L. *Shame and Pride.* New York: W.W. Norton, 1992.

——— ed. *The Many Faces of Shame.* New York: Guilford Press, 1987.

Olds, D. L., J. Eckenrode, C. R. Henderson, H. Kitzman, J. Powers, R. Cole, K. Sidora, P. Morris, L. M. Pettitt, and D. Luckey. "Long-term effects of home visitation in maternal life course and child abuse and neglect." *Journal of the American Medical Association* 278(1997):637–43.

Olds, D. L., C. R. Henderson, R. Cole, J. Eckenrode, H. Kitzman, D. Luckey, L. Pettitt, K. Sidora, P. Morris, and J. Powers. "Long-term effects of nurse home visitation on children's criminal and antisocial behavior." *Journal of the American Medical Association* 280(1998):1238–44.

Olds, David L., and Harriet Kitzman. "Can home visitation improve the health of women and children at environmental risk?" *Pediatrics* 86(1990):108–16.

Osofsky, Joy D. "Affective development and early relationships: Clinical implications." In *Interface of Psychoanalysis and Psychology,* edited by J. W. Barron, M. N. Eagle, and D. L. Wolitsky. Washington, DC: American Psychological Association, 1992, pp. 233–44.

Osofsky, J. D., D. M. Hann, and C. Peebles. "Adolescent parenthood: Risks and opportunities for mothers and infants." In *Handbook of Infant Mental Health,* edited by C. H. Zeanah, Jr. New York: Guilford Press, 1993, pp. 106–19.

Paley, Vivian Gussin. *You Can't Say You Can't Play.* Cambridge, MA: Harvard University Press, 1992.

Panel Reports. *International Journal of Psychoanalysis* 81(2000):141–65.

Panksepp, Jaak. *Affective Neuroscience: The Foundations of Human and Animal Emotions.* New York: Oxford University Press, 1998.

Papousek, H., and M. Papousek. "Cognitive aspects of preverbal social interactions between human infant and adults." In *Parent-Infant Interaction* (Ciba Foundation Symposium). New York: Associated Scientific Publishers, 1975.

Paradiso, S., R. G. Robinson, N. C. Andreasen, I. E. Downhill, R. J. Davidson, P. T. Kirchner, G. L. Watkins, L. L. B. Ponto, and R. D. Hichwa. "Emotional activation of limbic circuitry in elderly normal subjects in a PET study." *American Journal of Psychiatry* 154(1997):384–89.

Parens, Henri. *The Development of Aggression in Early Childhood.* New York: Jason Aronson, 1979.

Plutchik, Robert. *The Psychology and Biology of Emotion.* New York: Harper Collins, 1994.

———. *Emotion: A Psychoevolutionary Synthesis.* New York: Harper and Row, 1980.

———. *The Emotions: Facts, Theories, and a New Model.* New York: Random House, 1969.

Rapaport, David. "On the psychoanalytic theory of affects." *International Journal of Psychoanalysis* 34(1953):177–98.

Reiman, E. M., R. D. Lane, G. L. Ahern, G. E. Schwartz, R. J. Davidson, K. J. Friston, L. S. Yun, and K. Chen. "Neuroanatomical correlates of externally and internally generated human emotion." *American Journal of Psychiatry* 164(1997):918–25.

Rutter, Michael. "The interplay of nature, nurture, and developmental influences." *Archives of General Psychiatry* 59(2002):996–1000.

Schore, Alan N. *Affect Regulation and the Origin of the Self: The Neurobiology of Emotional Development.* Hillsdale, NJ: Lawrence Erlbaum, 1994.

Shapiro, Theodore. "The 41st international psychoanalytic congress. Santiago, Chile 1999: Foreword." *International Journal of Psychoanalysis* 80(1999):275–76.

Soref, A. R. "Narcissism: A view from infant research." *Annual of Psychoanalysis* 23(1995):49–77.

Spitz, Rene A. *No and Yes: On the Genesis of Human Communication.* New York: International Universities Press, 1957.

Stern, Daniel. "Affect attunement." In *Frontiers of Infant Psychiatry,* edited by J. D. Call, E. Galenson, R. L. Tyson. New York: Basic Books, 1984, pp. 1–14.

———. "The representation of relational patterns: Developmental considerations." In *Relationship Disturbances in Early Childhood,* edited by Arnold Sameroff and R. N. Emde. New York: Basic Books, 1989, pp. 52–69.

———. *The Interpersonal World of the Infant.* New York: Basic Books, 1985.

———. *The Motherhood Constellation: A Unified View of Parent-Infant Psychotherapy.* New York: Basic Books, 1995.

———. *The Diary of a Baby.* New York: Basic Books, 1990.

Taylor, G. J., R. M. Bagby, and J. D. A. Parker. *Disorders of Affect Regulation: Alexithymia in Medical and Psychiatric Practice.* New York: Cambridge University Press, 1997.

Thomas, Alexander, and Stella Chess. *Temperament and Development.* New York: Brunner/Mazel, 1977.

Tomkins, Silvan S. *Affect Imagery Consciousness (Volume I): The Positive Affects.* New York: Springer, 1962.

———. *Affect Imagery Consciousness (Volume II): The Negative Affects.* New York: Springer, 1963.

———. *Affect Imagery Consciousness (Volume III): The Negative Affects: Anger and Fear.* New York: Springer 1991.

———. *Affect Imagery Consciousness (Volume IV): Cognition: Duplication and Transformation of Information.* New York: Springer, 1992.

———. In *The Many Faces of Shame,* edited by Donald L. Nathanson. New York: Guilford, 1987, pp. 133–61.

Tucker, S. J. "The long-term efficacy of a behavioral parent training intervention for families with two-year olds." Doctoral dissertation, Rush University, DNS Program (1996).

Webster-Stratton, C. "Stress: A potential disruptor of parent perceptions and family interactions." *Journal of Clinical Child Psychology* 19(1990):302–12.

———. "What really happens in parent training?" *Behavior Modification* 17(1993):407–56.

Westman, Jack. *Licensing Parents: Can We Prevent Child Abuse and Neglect?* New York: Plenum Press, 1994.

Winnicott, Donald W. *The Maturational Processes and the Facilitating Environment.* New York: International Universities Press, 1965.

Zeanah, Charles H., Oommen K. Mammen, and Alicia F. Lieberman. "Disorders of attachment." In *Handbook of Infant Mental Health,* edited by C. H. Zeanah. New York: Guilford Press, 1993, pp. 332–49.

Zima, B. T., K. B. Wells, B. Benjamin, and N. Duan. "Mental health problems among homeless mothers." *Archives of General Psychiatry* 53(1996):332–38.

Index